IN THE EYE OF
EINSTEIN
ACCESSING YOUR HIGHER MIND

ELLIOT LAURENCE PhD
MINDMAVERICKS.ORG

The cover illustration is original artwork
derived from an impressionistic painting by
Elliot Laurence

IN THE EYE OF EINSTEIN

ACCESSING YOUR HIGHER MIND

Second Edition

CAN OUR VISIONS CREATE THE UNIVERSE OR DOES THE UNIVERSE CREATE OUR VISIONS?

Both can be true.

Access your higher mind, find out how and discover this hidden symbiotic relationship:

"In The Eye of Einstein"

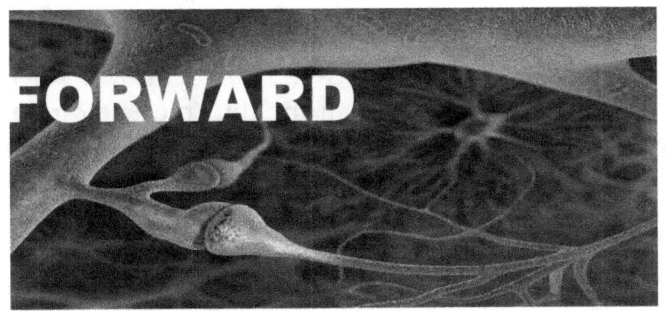

FORWARD

Psychologists are discovering more everyday how we humans have a duel capacity. We are habitual, living in a box, mechanical, organic machine-like beings; yet, we have the capacity to go beyond and think out of the box. We have the ability to envision and implement our visions.

There has been a constant battle throughout history, between two basic factions of humanity. Those who wish to maintain the status quo and don't make waves and those who make waves and stir things up. But the fact is that even in the most ideal situation, there will always be waves.

So why not make waves and learn how to surf over our waves, and the waves of others, without becoming immersed in them and lose our humanity.

A few people have woken up and have seen our mechanicalness. They have tried to get others to wake up too. Thus we have the Sages of time. But now, we have the biggest challenge of all that lie in front of us. This challenge is called the digital age.

The computer is seducing us into a whole new layer of the illusion of life; it makes us seem more superior through virtual reality. The irony is that we are already living in a virtual reality. In fact, when we learn to step away from this present virtual reality, we can see how the whole system of life and social engineering is utterly mechanical.

In the near future, there will be whole generations that will exist mainly through a computerized virtual world. This is easy to see today with all of the video games, Google Glass and Apps, up the yin-yang, on smart phones and such.

There needs to be a way to maintain and progress human conscious evolution and still make technology work for us, rather than making us work for it.

Our humanity is on the line here. Now don't get me wrong, I'm not against the wonders of technology. I am however, against the lack of conscious responsibility that goes along with it. There is complicity that people are allowing themselves to be lulled to sleep even deeper than they already are.

My job is to help people to first, become aware of this complicity and second, to provide a framework that can both capitalize on technology and provide tools for conscious evolution that can go beyond the current methods.

You might say I am teaching you how to win in the Star Trek movie's test called the "Kobayashi Maru." Where there seems to be a no win situation, but in fact you can win if you find a way to think out of the box and change the test's parameters.

CONTENTS

I

ABOUT THIS BOOK

The organization of sound creates music.

The organization of light creates art.

The organization of geometry creates architecture.

The organization of thought creates visionary thinking, inspiration and consciousness.

People such as Einstein, Leonardo da Vinci, Euclid, Copernicus, Galileo, Newton, Buddha etc., had the ability to tap into some greater force other than themselves. As a result, they were able to envision tremendous things that changed the world and its general consciousness.

Maybe you admire these people and you too, would like to find a way to become a visionary like they were. Maybe you would like to be an innovator yourself or, at the very least, be able to see the world and universe around you in a greater perspective.

But finding a reliable way to achieve a connection with this greater creative force in the universe is a different story.

The good news is:

This book is about the science of visionary thinking. It is a learning system that will enable you to experience forward visionary states of mind almost anytime you wish. You will also learn how to maintain these visionary states even in the midst of chaos and inspire others around you.

This is accomplished through Brain Games that train you how to achieve higher visionary states of mind and provide you with enough flight time in these states, to be able to do something while in them. You will also be able to find many other ways to achieve these higher conscious visionary states on your own.

It can also show you how to work with a team of people who wish to envision together, without the egos getting in the way. This factor in itself is very powerful. You can really make some changes in whatever you wish to do with many creative minds in sync.

These games contain a three pronged path which are:

ONE: Cleansing your magnetic field (mind, body and emotions).

People do this all the time already, but don't understand that they are doing this.

TWO: Channeling ideas, thoughts, visions through Holographic thinking.

Creative people do some of this often and some activities induce it, but again, do not necessarily realize what they are doing or why they are doing it.

THREE: Establishing a self identity as you the 'Observer' (which is separate from your body, heart and mind) and allows you to observe all of the cleansing and channeling, without getting immersed in what you see, feel or do.

This is something most, if not all, conscious raising practices promote, through meditation, yet limit you by requiring you to be under special ideal circumstances.

So how is visionary thinking taught?

As mentioned, when you meditate usually you need a special peaceful place to achieve a quiet, higher state of mind. But once you leave that perfect space, you have to deal with the chaos of life. What I have done is help you to organize certain thoughts for your meditation and developed brain games for you to play, that speeds up the chaos so that you are used to the chaos and become the calm eye of the storm or what I call an "Inner Body Experience." This is the experience of having a sense of self that is separate from your body, feeling or thought. It is "The Observer," something that transcends space and time.

Now when you are in the ordinary conditions of chaotic life, it is easier to maintain your composed meditative state. When you are in that ideal space of meditation, you will be able to achieve much more.

In fact, at this point in time, I actually thrive in more chaos.

Although these Brain Games are fun and humorous, they are seriously effective and have been successful on different levels for people from ages eight to eighty.

There may be many ideas you have heard before, but I will show you how to use these ideas in a whole new accelerated way and you will be able to achieve certain higher visionary states of consciousness almost immediately, where it would have taken other seekers of such states throughout history, years to accomplish.

The thing about great discoveries is that at first people did not necessarily find them to be remarkable. For example: Michael Faraday discovered the operating principal of an electromagnetic generator. It was inefficient and no one at that time could find a practical use for it. However as time went on, others came along and created the magnificent world of electrical gadgets that we have today.

I have discovered a way to achieve these higher visionary states of consciousness using a combination of elements that have been around for a while in one form or another. I have arranged them in a particular way through brain games that can induce these visionary states. They cannot only be achieved very quickly, but can be maintained under the chaotic circumstances of everyday life.

It is a combination of meditation principals, psychological alignment, reprogramming induced physiological responses and specific improvisational theater games.

These exercises and games break up mechanical thinking and make you think "out of the box." The first are exercises and personal mind-sets that you can do on your own. The second are ten games that need to be done in a group between four to twenty people (the more the merrier).

It is also important to note, that just doing these exercises once will only give you a taste. I suggest you do them with your group at least a dozen times, before you will begin to make a more permanent change to your mind and body. Moreover, if you do them consistently once a week, the benefits will amaze you, once a day, even more so.

Eventually, I hope you get a chance to experience a workshop with me someday. I would then train you how to do these and other games more effectively so you can show your own group how to do them.

This does not mean that working alone won't be effective. This book has many dimensions and can help you understand and apply the methods by which great innovators, like Albert Einstein, Leonardo da Vinci's and other's minds used in some form or another. But, a group has a whole other dynamic to it.

This has changed my life and many others around me and I hope it changes yours too.

THE 3 BASIC ELEMENTS OF THE CONSCIOUS VISIONARY PROCESS:

**BECOMING
THE OBSERVER**

**VISIONARY
EXPERIENCE**

**CLEANSING YOUR
MAGNETIC FIELD**

**CHANNELING
HOLOGRAPHIC
THINKING**

ONE: CLEANSING THE MAGNETIC FIELD

CHEMICALLY:
Diet, Fasting,
Fragrances,
Certain Chemicals,
Nature

CLEANSING MAGNETIC FIELDS:

ELECTRICALLY:
Laughter, Overcoming
Fear, Positive Emotions,
Sound / Music, Art,
Architecture and
Environment, Mental
Exercises, Acting
and Performing

MAGNETICALLY:
Movements,
Dance, Twirling,
Running, Walking,
Amusement rides,
Nature, Car Rides,
Drumming, Yoga
and Stretching

In order to not only be a visionary, but a more conscious being, we need to first cleanse our magnetic fields.

Cleansing and reorganizing our magnetic field makes us feel balanced and open to new things, including thinking in new ways. It helps to subdue the constant internal mind chatter. In Zen Buddhism it's called emptying your cup or becoming an empty canvas. Almost everyone wants to have this feeling and will go to great lengths to get there.

We are all electrochemical magnetic factories and give off a unique magnetic signature. If you change one factor, it affects the other two.

Here are some examples:

Changing your diet or fasting will alter your chemistry, in turn your mood (electrical charge) and your magnetic field alters due to the change in the electrical charge.

7

Laughter changes your electrical patterns, releases endorphins and alters your chemistry and magnetic field. That is why laughter has been reported to cure some people of disease.

If you take an iron rod and hit it against some concrete for a few moments, it will become magnetic, because all the electrons line up. So dancing, hiking, running, drumming, even driving through mountains, produces a change in your magnetic field. This translates to your electrical field and eventually your chemistry.

This is why the Whirling Dervish dancers spin their magnetic field against the more powerful magnetic field of the earth and why children like to do it so much. Roller coaster rides, skate boarding, racing, working out in the gym, etc. all do it too.

Music's vibrations can evoke a whole host of emotions, body movements and thoughts. It can change both electrical and magnetic fields at the same time. This is why music has been the most popular form of mind-altering drug throughout history.

Taking in beauty without the need to posses it changes your electricity, then chemistry, then your magnetic field.

This magnetic field cleansing is what makes us feel good. It clears away all the garbage floating around in our minds. It provides an empty canvas for the next step of higher thinking called channeling.

TWO: CHANNELING WAVELENGTHS

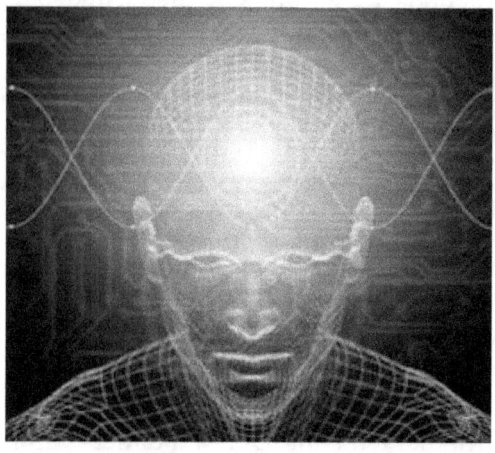

In quantum physics it has been discovered that everything is made up of waves. Researchers have discovered that even the smallest particles are made up of waves. There is actually no such thing as a solid. What is considered a solid is simply a force of resistance from one kind of force against another. This means that everything in the universe we presently know of is just a different kind of wave length.

The question then becomes, can we consciously feel these wavelengths and vibrate with them? We experience sound waves with our ears and body, light waves with our eyes and, if strong enough, as in the case of lasers, our bodies too. Then there are things like radio waves and infrared waves that we do not actually detect directly.

There are still other waves that our bodies can and do experience. With our own magnetic field, we can pick up vibrations of the other magnetic fields. The most common experience is sensing others' emotions and attractions. There are even more wave lengths we can pick up, maybe hundreds, thousands or millions. The actual numbers is presently hard to know, except that we do know a vast number exists.

Without the ability to understand and tap into what is called Morphic Fields, we are mostly living in blindness and deafness of the major portion of the sensory experience being given off by the universe. The level of profound sensory deprivation is equivalent to spending your life in a cave of total darkness and void of sound. The only things you become aware of are anything you accidently bump into. Yet the majority of people, for most if not all of their lives, live and die without having a clue about these other sensory experiences.

However, anyone who does anything creative over time will soon realize that ideas don't come from us, but through us. Each of us is a particular wave length receiver and sender, whether we realize it or not. Some channel art, others music, science, poetry, humor, etc. There are even people who specialize and can channel a particular kind of music and art.

When you hear crickets, birds, frogs or whatever, doing their mating sounds, they are also channeling Morphic Fields. It is a symbiotic relationship between their individual needs and the universe, composing and conducting the whole orchestration of sounds. There is little difference between those sounds and the sounds of any great composer. The only difference is the sophisticated, intelligent engineering of instruments and higher levels of emotions for which the music is composed. But to a female cricket, the sound of a male cricket's music sounds just as sweet as Bach's cantatas do to us.

All forms of life respond to different Morphic Fields, in their own way. I would also have to add that this is not limited to just life forms, at least the way we define them. When you view the electro/magnetic dance of the aurora borealis, you can see the same beat of movements that flocks of birds or bait balls of fish move to. The whole nature of magnetic fields is the vehicle of transference of cosmic waves to whomever or whatever is capable to receive them.

Einstein would channel astrophysics through space and time. That is where his ideas came from. The formulas came after his channeled experiences. He used his creative visionary imagination and ability to feel the kinds of vibrations that he was tuning into to visualize space, time and the whole lot.

Even our personalities are channeled. The entity that we actually are is not our personalities. Who we actually are as an entity, is simply that which observes our lives; as if we are viewing a play unfolding every day. Our personalities are the result of the particular choices we make starting from childhood. We imitate people we admire as we grow up and this adds up to the general mishmash adult package we claim to be us.

For example:

Elvis Presley was not Elvis Presley; he was just the first person to channel Elvis. Why? Because look at all the hundreds or even thousands of people channeling Elvis these days. Any actor understands this experience of channeling another person's personality. In fact if you are a good actor, you will even begin to think like the person you are channeling.

Here is an important thing:

Since there are so many different kinds of wave lengths to channel in so many different areas, if perchance, you are channeling something, it doesn't mean it is coming from God or spirits or a talking frog. There are creative wavelengths all around us all the time. They have been called by different names, but in the end they are simply cosmic wave lengths of a particular form of energy that we can tune in to. Now, just because you learned how to tap into a particular kind of wavelength, it doesn't make it divine providence. The universe gives us all kinds of ideas to select from. Just because it is a first idea that pops into your head, doesn't mean it is the ultimate idea from God. That is a limited reaction and your ego wants to jump and take claim for one idea in a sea of many ideas.

We know that radio waves can be used for all kinds of things: good, bad and everything in between. Channeling is the same thing. As a matter of fact we have examples throughout history of different people of every rank and file, taking their ability to channel something, calling it a message from God and slaughtering thousands, if not millions, of people.

Channeling is a tool like anything else. We also have to have consciousness and conscience to do something beneficial with it and to be respectful of other people who are interpreting what they channel.

The greatest value of the techniques presented here is that, when you do the Brain Games, you both cleanse your magnetic field and channel at the same time.

THREE: THE OBJECTIVE OBSERVER

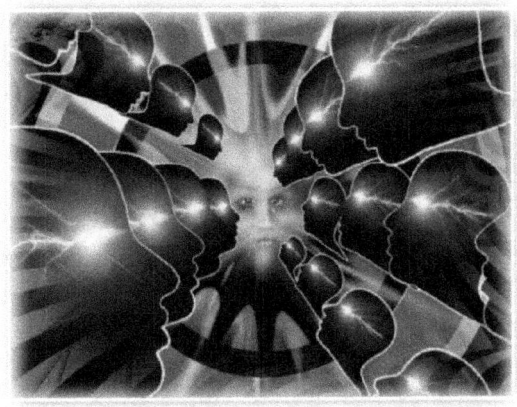

The biggest obstacle in being objective is the inability to keep from getting immersed in things. We lose ourselves in our relationships, our jobs, our favorite sports team, what country we live in and especially who we think we are.

When we do this, it becomes impossible to step back and see the bigger picture. Our identity is so tied up with "things" that we are unaware of our behavior and how it affects others, now and in the future. It may even affect our perception of the past, to some extent.

Being objective requires the ability to surf over life's circumstances and not get tripped up by the waves of complexity, not wipe out and not lose your sense of self. In other words: becoming a Mind Maverick, (a person who takes an independent stand; a non conformist), surfing over the maverick waves of the constantly changing circumstances of your life, in order to achieve your own life's purpose.

It is about looking beyond the surface of things, seeing micro expressions and going beyond the mask everyone wears, including our own.

Being immersed in just about anything is what causes wars, negative emotions, jealousy and fears and keeps us subjective. It takes special efforts to release yourself from this form of behavior, yet once you do, you will see the world very differently. If you want to understand how to improve your "reptilian human nature," you first have to discover what it is exactly and then go about changing it.

Let me also say that it is not an overnight process, but a lifelong process.

As Lao Tzu says; "Misfortune comes from having a body. Without a body, how could there be misfortune?"

There is no absolute conscious destination. Having absolute, finite consciousness and objective thinking is a common misconception. It is all a continuous journey till the day we leave our bodies and most likely beyond. Beware of anyone who claims they are above this identification and immersion. Of course one can be less immersed and more objective, but not completely so. You may be able to keep immersion in check, and react better and quicker in finding yourself immersed, but nonetheless getting immersed from time to time happens to all of us, especially when we least expect it.

There are different ways to detach yourself from immersion. There are the traditional ways, but what I hope to show you are some extremely quick ways using creativity which can keep you from getting so immersed in the first place.

As a bonus you will learn the secrets that can make you become more objective and expand the use of your brain.

INTELLIGENCE

Einstein said that "the difference between intelligence and stupidity is that intelligence has limits."

There are many different forms of intelligence:

There is the intelligence involving the memory and recollection of information and the calculation of it, emotional intelligence, inventive intelligence, instinctive intelligence, movement intelligence and visionary intelligence.

Even though it may be quite entertaining and popular, cleverness is a lower form of intelligence. Initially is very perceptive and can be cunning, but lacks any kind of meaningful use. It is usually used in advertizing and bringing attention to yourself, but also often with crime.

The most useful form of intelligence that I am talking about is conscious intelligence. It is visionary and objective thinking, intelligence and it requires the use of the right and left hemisphere of the brain simultaneously called, "Holographic Thinking.

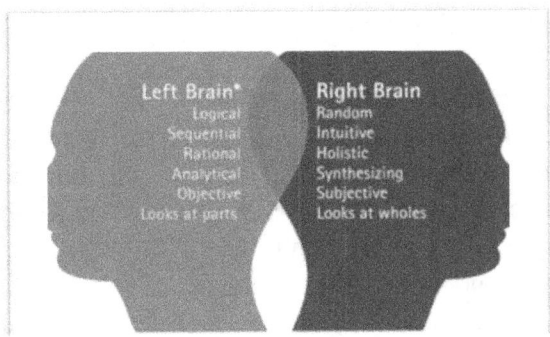

HOLOGRAPHIC THINKING

Holographic Thinking is learning to use both hemispheres of your brain simultaneously. It involves doing something mentally structured while simultaneously visualizing. A good example of this is perspective drawing; the discovery of perspective drawing was the major influence in creating the Renaissance.

Why?

Because, although some people in the past may have stumbled upon three dimensional thinking, the Renaissance was the first time in recorded history that you could teach other people how to think and visualize three dimensionally.

Thinking three dimensionally means that you are not so immersed in ideas. It also means that ideas are not linear but spherical blips on an interconnected web of interchangeable and re-arrangeable blips. Achieving this means you can stand back and observe your ideas separate from yourself. You can then bring in other ideas to compare, combine and create even more ideas like rearranging orbs of knowledge. You can see a sort of genetic structure to the ideas and how you can modify them.

It is like the difference between artists who paint what they see and those who can visualize what has never been seen before. There is a world of difference between two and three dimensional thinking.

WHY AREN'T PEOPLE ALREADY EDUCATED TO THINK CRITICALLY AND HOLOGRAPHICALLY?

With all the technology available to us today, it is important to realize that computers and machines will never be able to envision, imagine, perceive, channel and generate ideas, nor will they be able to teach you how to do so. To do such a thing, requires direct human to human interaction and the conscious retraining of the stimulus response mechanism in all of us. Yet our culture is being deluded and duped to think that this is still possible with technology.

For example certain websites claim to help you expand your brain. Well this is a half truth. They do speed up your brain and dilate some neural pathways, but the pathways developed are those of memory. Even better comprehension is still about memories, just a bigger collection of them. They do not teach you how to envision and think objectively. The neural pathways to that are in completely different parts of the brain. In fact, all those websites can do is show you how to imitate a computer and be faster at it. In other words all dressed up for thinking but nowhere to go. Now this does not mean that memory is not important, but it is not "thinking."

It is also important to understand that human to human interaction of brain training is irreplaceable and is the most important factor of human development. The ability to envision and think objectively <u>is</u> the defining principle of intelligent life. This separates us from any other living species and stops us being a totally mechanical one. With the momentum of enticing technological advances, it is the most crucial factor to get right in our lifetimes, or forever hold our peace.

We now have generation after generation of youth that are growing up immersed in the technological misconception that computing tools and accumulation of facts is critical thinking, and the educational system is contributing, if not driving, this debacle.

For example:

As was mentioned, the discovery of perspective drawing was so profound, it created the Renaissance.

Why?

Because it was the first time in recorded history, that so many people could be taught to think in three dimensions. Thinking in 3D translates to envisioning new ideas.

Now we have computer programs that create the 3D views for you automatically and, although there are unique opportunities in design than ever before, using automated programs sacrifices the greater process of a higher envisioning process that occurs when you have to construct and visualize things from scratch in your own mind.

The emphasis on math and science, to the exclusion of the arts and creativity, is a death knell of the greater human potential. As adults, we are being constantly wooed and bombarded by technology. Look at the lines for the new iPhones and Xboxes. See how the most successful films are about complete fantasy worlds and how in video games the visualization process of your own minds is replaced by other predetermined fantasies already spelled out for you.

It was hard enough to teach people how to activate their true thinking processes before all of this technology, now this lack of real thinking is almost becoming extinct. True thinking is something that every great philosopher and thinker of antiquity fought so hard to get us to do long before the world was flooded with the diversion of technology.

Yes, technology has brought us great things and is the results of some amazing thinking and innovation. I am far from being a Luddite myself, but those people who have and are doing the thinking are products of a more thinking age and/or are the exceptions to the general public. If we do not do something in the educational arena soon, real thinking, as rare as it is, will be even rarer and maybe reserved for a very small elite or simply be left to accident. This, in my opinion, is likely to contribute to the downfall of humanity, more than wars, not recycling or not developing renewable resources.

Real thinking is not the accumulation of more and more information and the associative properties of that information. Thinking is a whole other process, that makes our minds step back and objectively observe information, visualize, and bring in ideas outside of ourselves and see how to relate them to not only other ideas, but to ideas that have not even been thought of yet. We need to be able to connect to the source of ideas outside of ourselves, and have the foresight of someone like Dmitri Mendeleev, who drafted the first periodic table and knew to leave some spaces open for elements yet to be discovered. Then there are others who have discovered something new about science and had to face the ridicule of their contemporaries. Their thinking was so inspired and compelling that they were willing to face the slings and arrows of outrageous fortune to stand behind it. That is real thinking.

There are also different kinds of thinking. There is the thinking derived from your instincts, movements, emotional intelligence as well as ideas and concepts that come from your intellect. Above all that, there is visionary thinking.

So where do you go to learn how to actually think and visualize; not just memorize and calculate? As I mentioned, schools are not teaching this, computers and the so called brain training websites are not teaching it. Maybe in some more advanced higher learning classes in ethics and philosophy people might be challenged to think about things differently. The new "common core" programs are just doubling down on the same old process of teaching and have little to do with thinking and certainly not teaching one how to be a visionary. Up until now there has not been an actual method that is specifically designed to teach you not just the different processes of learning and expanding your learning capacity, but how to visualize solutions and utilize what you have learned at the same time.

This is where the value of this book comes into the picture. You will learn about the different thinking processes, how to access them and set priorities of different levels of thinking.

I pointed out earlier that it is not just the formal school systems that are focusing on memorizing and calculating, and lots of programs outside of the formal school system that can improve your memory, help you calculate faster and fill your head with more and more mind cluttering information.

This is because the established school system only knows how to teach this way. It is harder to find, except in bits and pieces, the knowledge associated with objective thinking, creativity and visionary thinking. The ability to physically expand and use more of the creative brain has not been developed as a scientific teaching method, nor has it been truly encouraged. Any results of creative thinking are mostly accidental and/or rely on the hope of naturally talented people. In fact, the whole teaching system does more to promote self judgment and low self esteem, due to its attitudes and grading system. This is especially true if a student's thinking is different than the norm.

How can students be encouraged to think differently if no one taught the teachers how to? In most cases, teachers who breakaway from the traditional system of teaching, are considered strange and are admonished for doing so. Only in rare cases, under unusual circumstances, has a teacher been rewarded and encouraged for unique teaching methods.

In fact, it is so rare to find a teacher who was allowed to be bold and teach their unique methods of teaching, that there have been movies made about them. This uniqueness should not be rare, but the expected.

The new popular websites still do not teach you how to think critically. They ask you to respond to a problem or game of their construct. You have to play in the context of their games. You still are asked to fit into their system.

If you think "out of the box" you cannot change the parameters of the problems they present or get new inspiring solutions. The games are not about new ideas. They offer the same old approach to learning, just dressed up in a computer program. They do not encourage you to delve deep into your creative, visionary mind.

As of late, computer programs cannot adjust and understand your unique "out of the box" solutions. They also do not teach you how to be an observer, separate from yourself and all that goes on. They do not teach you how to visualize like Einstein and all the other great innovators throughout time.

Einstein did not memorize all kinds of information, but he did have a grasp on concepts and knew where to go to fill in the technical blanks to support his visions. This freed his mind to look at a bigger picture.

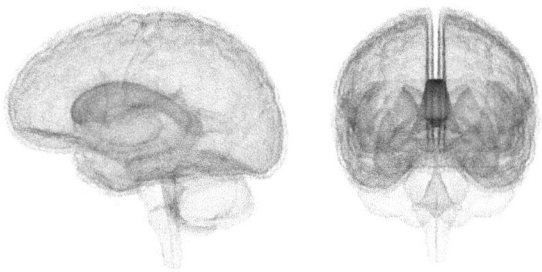

To think in new ways, requires both psychological and physiological changes. The psychological changes include learning how to not think mechanically. The physiological changes involve the dilation of the neural pathways and thickening of the Corpus Callosum, (the bridge between both halves of the brain). Thinking in new ways can show you how to process information, connect its value and create new ways of looking at that information, as well as its possible application to whatever you choose.

We could argue about each of our own subjective philosophies and semantics till the cows come home, but how can we be more objective about such things so we are able to verify or evaluate any philosophy or practice before committing to something?

You cannot put rocket fuel into a car engine and expect it to function better. You will most likely blow it up. You need to put rocket fuel into a rocket engine for it to be utilized properly. So how can we turn our brains that are like a car engine to become a rocket engine?

Wouldn't you agree that any such ability would be immeasurable in value? It would mean that whatever you used as your philosophical guide, you would be operating with a highly functioning mind and not filling your mind with just any information with a mind that is open to subjective interpretation. That is why it is important to open up, dilate neural pathways, and gain more access to the objective mind.

IS THIS ABOUT SPIRITUALITY?

No! For the purpose of this Brain Training, you do not have to have a spiritual inclination, nor is there any advantage to having a Spiritual Path one way or another. This is about seeing and understanding with a scientific eye. How you wish to fill yourself with the content of your interests is your business.

Some experiences derived from the Brain Exercises, could be associated with higher states of consciousness created in spiritual practices. But you could make the same claim about breathing too. What is important is to understand that as you continue to expand your brain, certain experiences considered to be spiritual are demystified and revealed to show their scientific physiological and psychological natures.

There are all kinds of spiritual practices and scientific theories that approach this subject. But who are we to evaluate what these theories and practices mean in the first place, if we need to discover who we truly are and develop the intelligence at the highest level and interpret whatever knowledge, theories and experiences we are trying to understand?

Even if an ant had the consciousness to know that there was something going on that was much bigger than itself, how much could it actually know with its limited brain capabilities beyond fears of The Giant Rainstorm God? The same goes for us. What is better, having the use of a pebble size portion of your brain or a bowling-ball-size portion of your brain to understand the world around us?

How is it not the most important thing we can do to increase our mental / emotional / perceptive capabilities, instead of just believing things?

Other than blithering idiots, most people would agree that there is a necessity to increase the abilities of the mind. The problem is not so much the understanding of the need to do it, but the "how to do it," especially since there is no real institutional training on how to actually learn. Conventionally, there are subjects to learn about facts and how to compare them. Until now, there has been nothing that teaches you how to actually engage and increase the learning process, or even how to critically think about what you just learned in the first place.

Outside of the institutional learning arena, brain training is presently a ninety million dollar industry, so there is obviously an attempt being made. But if you actually analyze what is being taught, it is still memorization of facts and the increased speed of that memory and not actually thinking.

The ability to step back and see things from a more objective vantage point is not the focus at all, nor is it anywhere in sight. Any real experience of objectivity is purely accidental.

The other major thing is that we are stimulus response machines. We react to stimuli and we do so in mechanical ways that we learned by accident and not through intentional thought as to the why and how we are reacting so. In order to be able to really think and not react unconsciously, we first have to see how we are mechanical, and then retrain ourselves to not respond in such a fashion. This all leads to the understanding of the limitations of what is called "Formatory Thinking" or form thinking.

Thinking is not the accumulation of facts and mechanical association of them to any given subject. Actual thinking is a whole different process and it occurs in a different part of the brain than memorization. In fact, there are many different ways of thinking and they require accessing many different parts of the brain; the individual parts as well as the whole brain simultaneously. In this book, you will be exposed to these ways of thinking and ways to access these corresponding parts of the brain. It will mean learning how to detect whole new sensations and / or recognizing those you are already experiencing.

You will also learn how to connect with other people and nature in an entirely new way, called Morphic Resonance, as presented by Dr. Rupert Sheldrake. You will also discover it is possible to connect with the mind set of people who are no longer living. This is because they are still connected to this Morphic Life Energy Field, along with their ideas they introduced to the world and how they conceived them to begin with. This is because everything is connected in some way or another.

Ideas great and small are merely an electrical impulse or series of impulses traveling on a filament that is part of a greater complex web of electrical filaments. The universe structurally looks like our brains neural pathways, so the mind and universe mirror each other. This is being discovered everyday in the world of astrophysics, to the point that there is a strong indication that we both receive and transmit the messages of the cosmos all the time and at the same time. What we experience as a three dimensional universe is possibly a kind of a holographic binary code described on the outside membrane of the whole universe itself.

In other words:

Our visions create the universe and the universe creates our visions.

This also means that you can tap into this vast connected array of filaments from your own back yard and eventually catch up to the stream of thought of those who have traveled that stream before you. They made it easier to catch up with them now, because they have already blazed the path of how to get there.

So the intelligence acquiring process is like the esoteric symbol of the snake eating its own tail. We want to gain more intelligence, but, we need to use more physical brain to actually gain more intelligence, and we need more intelligence to gain more brain.

As you read, you will see how these ideas are doable and can be practically applied and are not just flowery theoretical ideas. You will see how people like Einstein, Leonardo, Galileo, etc., tapped into their ideas and, more importantly, you can too. You even do it already to some degree and just need to learn how to recognize it.

DOING, NOT JUST TALKING

Just because a person can speak eloquently, doesn't make them more intelligent. In fact, the media is filled with these kinds of people. Just look at the news or who has their own TV show. Why do you think we have the kind of government that we have? In fact, throw in an English accent and you have the perfect storm for being duped. Our present society values fluff and duff over substance.

Although it has tremendous value at times, just quoting the results of some great person's profound thoughts, does not mean you have done the critical thinking yourself. It may evoke some thinking in you, but thinking critically about something from scratch, without much influence, is a whole different order of thinking.

Just relying on a diet of sound bites of knowledge and cute sayings, is simply not going to effect change in your consciousness. It may make you a bit more alert about a particular subject for a few seconds, or a minute at best.   .

If you think these sound bites will change your being, you are only fooling yourself. In some ways, it is worse than having no sayings of knowledge at all, because it perpetuates the illusion of personal work on changing yourself.   .

Truly evolving and making significant changes in yourself and your consciousness, requires going into more depth in your research and reading. It requires deeper work on yourself, facing your fears, resisting your mechanical behavior, transforming suffering and not avoiding it.

It also means that thinking and/or wishing to be rewarded materially for your inner beings development is a complete misdirection.

Admiring those that have achieved great material success from their so called spiritual work, simply because they have achieved material success, is simply materialism and has nothing to do with self development and higher thinking. If they are promising you health and wealth as the affirmation of you following their program, run away as fast as you can.

"Keep your eyes in your sockets; they have their hands in your pockets,"

CONSCIOUS INSPIRATION

Everyone is capable of doing extraordinary things. Some people do simple things extraordinarily and some do complex things extraordinarily. In any case, the key is that they love what they do and they are inspired to do it. Some of you may have talent; some have inspiration, yet others an overwhelming desire. Both talent and inspiration is like money you find on the street. It's great when you find it, but you can't depend on it. It is better to have a strong desire and a method that can bridge the gaps between moments of inspiration and, in turn, compensate for lack of natural talent, until that next moment of inspiration strikes.

Show me your desire to do something, and I will show you how to get there.

By learning the methods of thinking presented here and accessing your higher mind, you will learn a system that will enable you to think and perform innovatively, whether you feel like it or not. As an additional benefit, it actually increases the frequency of your inspirational moments.

The essence of this higher type of thinking can be called; "Conscious Inspiration." This means that not only can you be inspired, but you have tools to help you be inspired more often, and the ability to step back and observe, while all this is going on.

Think of a time you have been inspired about something or someone; you were selfless and were doing what needs to be done without ego trying to stake a claim. When you are in the state of inspiration, the "you" is not the body; "you" are a more alive conscious entity that is separate from your body observing the show called "your life."

INSIGHT

Long ago, I learned that each person has to fulfill his or her own destiny. Be it politics, religion, physics, mayonnaise-making, etc. I have no interest in filling others brains with my brand of nonsense. But what I can do is show others how to expand their minds so that whatever they choose to fill it with will be viewed with their highest intelligence.

After forty years of formal education, dedicated research and proven life experiences, I feel confident to boldly present and defend this information. Being very down-to- earth, I learned how to question anything and verify everything. If I include theoretical information, it will be stated as such.

The ideas presented here are not wishful thinking or another New Age sugar pill. You are going to be given proven methods that will actually increase your ability to use more of your brain. These ideas are the consolidations of research of how history's great minds and even great contemporary minds work.

As a result, you will find that there will be other benefits such as more conscious awareness, objective thinking, perceptiveness and the use of many other faculties.

Although you can get insight and tools to work with on your own (from this information and exercises presented to you in this book), there is still no replacement for having a direct interactive experience in a group workshop. Working on your own is much slower. We cannot see ourselves objectively, we need feedback from the outside from a trusted person who knows how to interpret what it is that we are experiencing. Each of us needs "in the moment" observations and contributing ideas, to prime the pump of the mind and to help us expand our perceptions. Everyone needs a mentor of some kind from time to time, or at least for a little while.

THE MULTIPURPOSE OF THIS INFORMATION

There are actually two levels of which the information in this book can be used. The first level is to improve your practical life. The second is to begin to understand and experience a higher form of conscious existence and become a visionary.

As you read, you will see how this is more than brain training, but thinking about it as brain training is a good start.

So what could be the potential benefits of what you can learn from this training?

In business, it might mean creating a new business or a way to change your existing business, finding a new effective marketing strategy, hiring the right person and consultants or making better investments, etc.

In your personal life, it might mean: minimizing conflict, increasing self discipline, recognizing your natural strengths and weaknesses, getting out of denial and/or facing your imperative issues and fears.

It has been shown that even simple brain training that makes your brain more active can help avert the onslaught of Alzheimer's disease and, in the case of children, help them to develop their brains much faster and more comprehensively. In all cases, it means stepping away from the maddening crowd, tapping into one's own self confidence and uniqueness and seeing oneself and humanity from a more advantageous perspective.

To add to the mix of benefits, according to psychologist Kelly McGonigal, studies have shown that people who believe that stress is bad died from stress at a rate of 43 percent more than those who took stress in their stride. Those who didn't believe that stress was bad actually had the lowest risk of dying, even over people who had little stress.

The statistics showed that the belief of stress being bad for you ended up being the fifteenth largest cause of death, more than skin cancer, AIDS and homicide. Transferring the physiological-stress response into challenging action, rather than being defeated by it, was a key to longevity.

Another study found that people under stress who chose to help others under that condition, actually had less stress and had more resilience.

Some of the practical benefits of the Brain Training methods in this book will help you to deal with pressure and stress better.

The higher levels of brain training will show you how to develop your consciousness, disclose hidden senses, see life from a more objective perspective, cut through the smoke and mirrors of mystical experiences in life, know when you are being duped by someone and bring clarity to your own knowledge of self.

I once had a mentor who said; "If you have to explain beauty to someone, then they will never be able to understand it." I feel the same about increased intelligence, that if a person does not understand and appreciate the value of gaining greater intelligence, they will never understand the value of that no matter what you can say or do.

WHY THINK LIKE EINSTEIN?

What would you say to someone who asked you each of the following questions?

1. Why do you need to see, if you have great hearing?

Maybe nothing, but the more faculties we acquire for our perceptions of life, the more we gain richness and understanding to our lives.

2. If, by doing certain things you could develop an additional sense to experience life, would you? Depending on what degree of commitment?

Wouldn't you like to have an opportunity to become more than what you are?

3. Wouldn't you like to experience inspiration more often?

Who does not enjoy inspiration? Why would a person not do all they could to live a more inspired life?

4. Why would you want to be a follower rather than a leader?

I would think you would want to be your own person and make your own deliberate decisions, if for no other reason than to not jump off a cliff like everyone else.

The answers to those questions are what define a higher thinking minded person from a fearful one. Yes, there are different degrees of commitment and everyone seeks comfort, but there is sort of a line where, if it came down to a life defining decision, that you would have to choose? Would you choose more consciousness at the expense of comfort in a given critical situation, or would you opt for comfort and denial of some truths?

Another big reason to develop your higher mind may not even be for you, but for the sake of educating the next generations, to show them how to be innovators and think critically. We have a lot of youth growing up just flipping a switch or clicking a mouse and expecting things to work. They feel entitled to have things work a certain way. There are waves of designers in all fields that cannot design without a special computer program to help them out. Although what can be created without critical thinking seems amazing, it is a recipe for eventual mediocrity.

There are even more reasons to exercise the brain.

Every day we are discovering how exercising the brain can postpone aging and Alzheimer's disease. It can also help with more coordination and multitasking. At the very least, increasing more neural pathways to your brain can help you to become your own person and not an automaton or just another bait fish waiting to be consumed by a higher order of predator fish.

UNIQUE BRIAN TRAINING

As far as brain training goes, the methods in this book are not taught anywhere else. Yes, there are some well intended computer programs, sound, light and/or energy contraptions that attempt to approach what is presented in this book. These methods are fragmented though. They do not give you the whole picture and you cannot depend on them. You would only be able to use the enhanced brain functioning they offer while actually using those programs or contraptions, and thus not in the ordinary chaotic experiences of life. They do not change you permanently. Change comes from consistent conscious efforts from within and the knowledge of how to make those changes.

Relying on those methods would be as if you were in a space ship heading to a star a few light years away, but with a trajectory that was off by a millionth of a degree. For a long time you would think you were heading in the right direction, but when you actually arrived, you would find yourself light years off course.

As Socrates said: "It is far more difficult to disprove the truth with a little lie in it, than an absolute lie."

This is not to say that the people involved with these programs or contraptions are lying, but they only have fragments and are generally misinformed, misdirected and it may be a case of the well intentioned blind leading the blind.

In this business, it is vital to not depend on anything external, at least not for long. You need to see the whole of how things work from your own self understanding, so you are in control and can adjust your course. Each person's course is specific for them and they need to self-adjust to get them to their desired destination. You have to become a truth hitch-hiker, jumping from vehicle to vehicle not getting distracted by any particular vehicle and stay with one just because it's so shiny and comfortable.

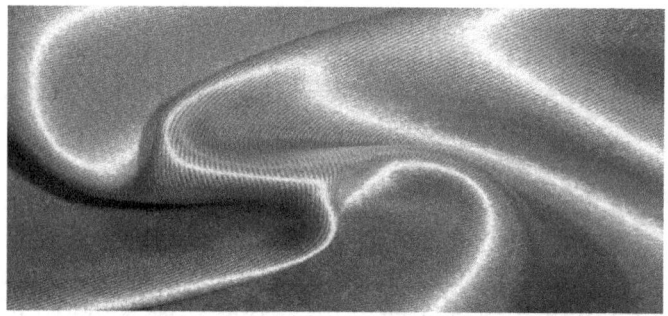

WHY DON'T PEOPLE THINK ON A MORE OBJECTIVE LEVEL NATURALLY?

To think on a more conscious objective level requires getting out of one's mental comfort zone. There are actual physiological reasons for the resistance to doing this, which I will discuss later. Through the ordinary conditioning of life, we learn how to think a certain way, and, when we learn something new, our first reaction is to fit new ideas into our old way of mechanical thinking. Few people learn how to actually think in a new way. They do not even understand the concept of thinking differently.

The other problem is: people walk around generally unaware of themselves even existing. They are daydreaming or preoccupied with their problems. If you go over to them and ask, "Are you aware right now?" In that moment they actually will be and say, "Yes," but then go back to their unaware state.

You might also ask: "What about just being happy with love and compassion?"

Well, love and compassion are a good default for the human condition, but they are just a place holder for gaining more consciousness. Yes absolutely, love and compassion are necessary, especially for an intelligent person. A person lacking that ingredient would most be likely a sociopath.

Why?

Because without love and compassion, what would be your motivation to do things in life? Most likely it would be your own selfish desires.

History is full of highly intelligent people who used all their faculties to do horrific things to other humans as a result of a damaged or nonexistent conscience.

We also live in a paradigm where just being a good person does not further evolution. Simply marching in place as a good person will not accomplish the task of the survival of the fittest. The actual survival of the fittest for humans also means the evolution of the fittest.

Why?

Because the conditions of life on Earth and the universe for that matter are constantly changing and we need to at least adapt to these conditions, if not try to stay ahead of them.

WHAT IS THE EXPERIENCE OF OBJECTIVE CONSCIOUSNESS?

First of all, it is important to understand that whatever is said about consciousness, it is a moving target and it is similar to taking a snapshot of a passing speeding train. One way to describe it is the same way I define art:

When I was teaching at the Academy of Art University, in San Francisco, I would often go up to the white board and draw something like this:

I would afterward ask the students, "What is this?"

They would joke around with me, but it was obvious and everyone agreed that it was simply a scribble. Then I would draw something around it and sign my name and date at the bottom like this:

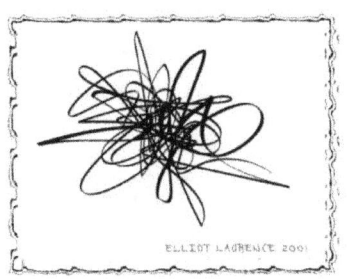

I would ask them again; "What is it now?" They would answer; "Art"

What changed? It was still the same scribble, yet how they viewed it was different.

How?

It is because now there was juxtaposition, a different frame of reference to it (literally). So a way to define art is not so much the actual creation itself, but the way it makes your mind step back and see what was done from a more insightful position.

This is how to view consciousness too, constantly stepping back in our minds eye and to frame, reframe and again reframe our lives and the universe around us.

Remembering to do this we can all potentially look at the world fresh and new every moment of every day, if we so chose.

OUR CONDITIONING

We are conditioned all of our lives to learn, see, react, behave and, most of all, think in a prescribed way. This sometimes results in not being able to "see the forest through the trees." However, some people don't fit into the acceptable ways of thinking. As these people make their way through life, they can be revered, but in many cases are scorned, at least at first, like Copernicus or Galileo, who had to break through sociological norms and other tremendous obstacles for their visions.

When we look back in history, we admire their tenacity and what they did to contribute to humanity. Even with that kind of admiration in mind, we still might find ourselves dismissing someone right in front of our own noses, in our own daily lives that has great new ideas to offer. Worst yet, our own capabilities and perceptions.

Stepping away from the crowd to see life from a different perspective, means learning how to find the self-confidence to both develop and trust your own perceptions.

This means not dismissing our own perceptions and capabilities which lie beneath the surface or flick quickly by like micro expressions.

Although meditation has been proven to be an amazing tool for accessing deeper parts of your psyche, it requires you to do this in a controlled quiet place or under some prescribed conditions of your choosing. However, life happens in chaos and we need to be able to respond to things mostly on the fly. The brain training in this book includes learning how to effectively observe yourself and meditate not only in a quiet space, but in the midst of chaos too, while walking, running and even fighting, just as Marcus Aurelius and Socrates were able to observe themselves even in battle.

Here are some successful entrepreneurs who used and still use meditation for building the successes of their endeavors: Steve Jobs (now deceased), The Beatles, David Lynch, John Mackey of Whole Foods, basketball coach Phil Jackson, and musician Leonard Cohen. They took time out of their day to find a quiet place to meditate and were able to take that awareness into their daily flow.

Now think what you could do if you were able to meditate most of your waking hours. Think about the powerful effects that it could have.

This is precisely what is so unique about the methods presented here. You get brain games that will show you how to speed up your brain to increase your multitasking capabilities, while remembering to keep a sense of yourself. You can both meditate and function in your everyday chaotic lives at the same time. You become the calm eye of the hurricane.

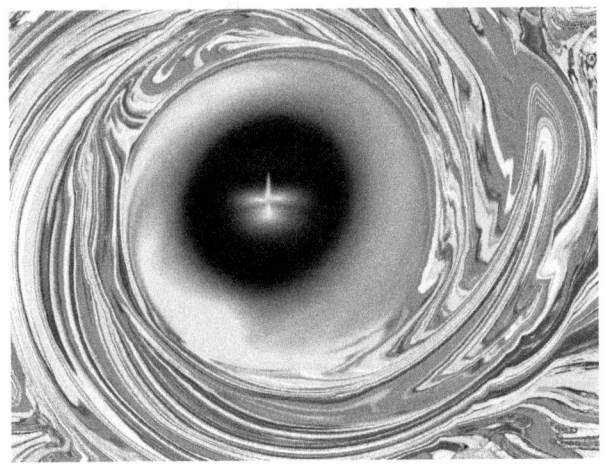

SELF IMPRESSION

We all get a self impression from the social conforming and conditioning in life that contributes to an imaginary picture of ourselves. This influences our judgment of our strengths and weaknesses. This has been prescribed for us all throughout our lives through our social conditioning from parents, friends, school and media. This is what makes us want to fit in.

In some cases it might make you believe you can't because someone told you so and, in other cases, you might harbor an inflated ego.

When the conditioning is negative, it will tend to make you settle for an unfulfilled, mediocre life.

In the case of an inflated ego, at some point it may propel you to do things you would never have done without that encouragement. On another level, it might make you so self-centered that may impede you.

It is important to find a true picture of yourself. In order to do this, you have to get over the need for approval from others and doing things in order to be liked.

In fact, the more a person demands the attention of others, the lower their self esteem. The more you feed that kind of behavior in those attention seekers, the more of a disservice you are doing them and their potential conscious evolution.

HOW DO I KNOW THIS IS HOW EINSTEIN THOUGHT?

Let me explain it this way:

Let's say you start to drive from Florida to California. While you are on this journey, you begin to notice specific things: there are certain rest stops; there is a detour through the Grand Canyon; there are some roads that have distinct features. One day you read about how another person had experiences that paralleled yours. That would be a good indicator that the other person traveled on the same road.

This is how I know how people like Einstein, Leonardo and Galileo, etc., thought. This is also how I know that if you do the brain games and exercises regularly; you too will begin to see things in more conscious visionary way and tap into the thoughts of all the great minds across space and time.

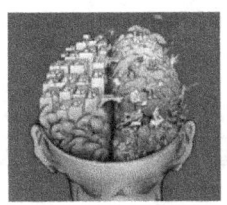

THE SECRET OF EINSTEINS BRAIN

When Einstein died, as many people know, his brain was preserved and dissected. A new study published on September 24, 2013, reveals that the two hemispheres in Einstein's brain were unusually well connected. Compared to most people's, Einstein's corpus callosum was thicker in many areas, indicating greater connectivity between his brain's two hemispheres and this has been linked with higher levels of intelligence.

This was so exciting for me to learn as it vindicated everything that I have been doing with the brain studies, experimentation and how I had been leading my life throughout the years. It is all about the simultaneous union of creativity and intellectual skills.

You see, Einstein was not so much an intellectual genius as he was a creative genius and a visionary. He himself said that "Imagination is more important than knowledge."

In fact, the greatest contribution that Einstein made to the world was not his specific contributions to science, however great, but his creative visionary process that most, if not all, astrophysicists use today.

WHAT DOES IT MEAN TO THINK LIKE EINSTEIN?

Someone who can think like Einstein is someone who can think more objectively and on a higher order, who thinks for himself/herself, who questions everything, who is not satisfied with typical answers, who can think "out of the box."

These people challenge "Formatory (form) Thinking" or myopic thinking in themselves and others. They can deal with difficulty in their lives more easily, let go of what no longer works, reinvent themselves and keep up with the changes that inevitably occur in life.

Such people think to some degree or another, that this is how they are already, but very few have actually learned these skills. This can be easily demonstrated by experiencing the specially developed brain challenges that I devised and seeing how well you do. Even with some skills in this area, everyone still needs constant practice, challenges and feedback to help us out of our subjective formatory world. For those that have some of these skills naturally, it is also important for them to know what they know and not simply rely on it intuitively. It is important to intentionally and consciously develop the skills further.

PRACTICING THE STUDY OF
THE HIGHER VISIONARY MIND

"It is our creativity, art and vision that separate us from the other creatures in this world. Why isn't that the most important form of education?"

The study of expanding your mind, and the ability to think and be an innovator like Albert Einstein and Leonardo da Vinci, means stepping away from the crowd, learning how to think in new ways, and having it be fun and humorous. The only thing required to learn this new way of thinking is your commitment to do so.

So I ask you, if all you had to do was make a small daily effort, would you?

The fact is that this is all possible, and, when you learn how to do so and recognize what is going on, you will find it is simple and obvious.

Although most people say that they would want to learn how to think like Einstein, few actually will make the effort.

Why is that?

It is because of fear of the unknown, no matter how simple and nonthreatening.

It is because of self-judgment.

It is because of habits and a lazy mind.

Even though acquiring this new mental power is simple, you still have to make an effort to do so. If you do decide to make this effort, you will be able to create a momentum that could last for the rest of your life.

You see, once the nuclear reaction is turned on, there is no turning back, and you will become a permanent mind explorer or what I call a Mind Maverick.

The difficulty is that what I am attempting to describe to you is the same thing as trying to describe the taste of a unique experience of vanilla. There is nothing else that can compare with that vanilla taste, so it can only be understood by experiencing that particular flavor. It is a base flavor or, in this case a base experience, against which other things are compared.

In general, people hear new ideas and try and fit them into their old way of thinking. Not everything can be compared to the taste of chicken. Sometimes things have their own taste and we have to learn what those tastes are. You cannot be an innovative thinker if you think you know what everything tastes like.

Another aspect is that learning how to use your brain like Einstein is an acquired taste. When you try it at first, it is like tasting something unusual for the first time. In the same way that your tongue tastes something and registers it in your brain, the mind itself has a tongue called the pineal gland, which also has to sort out the new sensations before the rest of our body and feelings have to decide to like it or not.

As in the event horizon of a black hole, we can only see the intensity of light and matter as it approaches the hole, but what actually happens in the black hole is a mystery to the outside observer.

It is not possible to accurately describe the experience in another dimension to someone while you are trying to experience it from a lower dimension. One can only talk about its effects and what might happen as you approach it. However, once you have the experience and are able to understand what that experience is, then although words are still inadequate, you share a common bond of understanding with others who experience it.

It is similar to trying to explain what a three dimensional sphere is as it passes through a two dimensional world to someone living in a two dimensional world. They would first see a dot appear from nowhere, which would grow to a circle and then became a dot again and disappear. There would be no possible concept of the totality of what a sphere is, if the person who only has a two dimensional way of viewing it and has no other way to perceive the world.

Unfortunately, there are some people that are simply not wired to see in three dimensions. Even worse; there are some people who only see in one dimension. It is very difficult to get them to see the world any differently than their wiring will allow. If they really worked at it, they possibly could eventually see in three dimensions, but they just have too much overwhelming fear of letting go of their prescribed reality and that keeps them back.

Trying to describe an experience of three dimensional thinking, when most people are thinking in two or one dimensions is quite difficult. One can describe some benefits of it, but not the broader actual interactive experience of it.

A good example of people who have been able to change their perspective is in the study of both quantum physics and astrophysics:

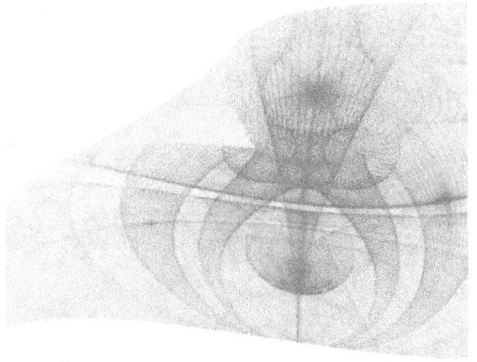

There had been a discussion about "string theory" for a long time. It was thought that all matter behaved like waves on vibrating strings. But there was a disagreement about how many dimensions existed. Some said ten; some said eleven; and all of the physicists had a different picture of how these strings looked and how they vibrated. Then someone stepped back and saw that they were not looking at a string, but that they were only seeing profiles of multi-facetted membranes intermingling, as if looking at the shadows of waving flags overlapping each other.

 What happened was that, although they were talking about other dimensions, they were still thinking in two dimensions. So when someone eventually stepped back, they could see that what they were looking at were three dimensional membranes. This exponentially changed and unified their conflicting perceptions.

It was like those 3D stereogram posters, where you have to look at a pattern a certain way and eventually an image appears right out of the flat graphic image that you first see.

Here is an example:

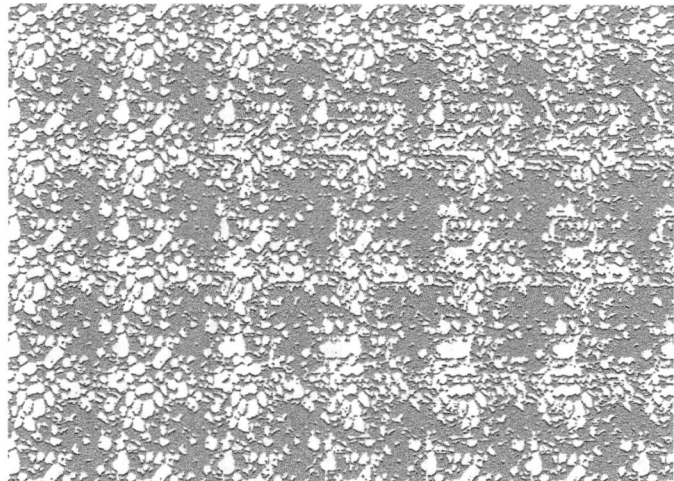

1. Stare at this as if you are looking beyond the plane of the paper to see a hidden spiral.

The other challenge in understanding three dimensional or Holographic Thinking is that, although I can create the other-dimensional experience in the mind for others, each person experiencing it needs to acquire a conscious taste or understanding of what it is that they are actually experiencing and what part of them is doing the experiencing.

There could also be some confusion as to how I am defining dimensions and how one typically thinks about them. In physical science, dimensions have actual physical properties. What I am talking about are psychological dimensional properties. It is a way to be separate from ideas and see all eleven dimensions as if they are interactive filaments all floating in a different kind of space and time and having separate realities. It also means not just stepping back once and seeing things differently, but stepping back over and over again.

It is like the difference between how color works as a solid paint as opposed to how color works as light. In the solid paint world, all colors combined create black. In the world of light, all colors create white light. The dimensional world I am talking about would be the equivalent of the world of light as opposed to solid paint. Although M-theory stands for *membrane theory*, M-theory for me stands for *mindbrane* theory.

The best way to describe this state of mind is the experience of when you are inspired. You could say that I am showing how to attain a state of inspiration on a more regular basis through the reverse engineering of inspiration and its effect on the body, emotions, mind and spirit.

In order to do this, one has to experience enough flight time in the experience to gain the consciousness about it. It is like making it to the top of a mountain. On your first attempt to climb, the path you are on seems like the only one. But once you get to the top, you can look down and see all the different ways of getting there.

It took me twenty-five years to understand how this process works, because there was no one to guide me on this particular path. Since I know what it is now, I can intentionally create the experience and guide people through it, so they can sort out what exactly it is they are experiencing much more quickly. Now it may only take anywhere from one to maybe four sessions for the individual I am guiding through the experience to get a basic understanding. How each person makes enough neural connections between both halves of their brain to realize and interpret the experience, is unique to them.

In any case, one session or four sessions, to get the basic idea one must still spend enough flight time in the experience through continually playing the Brain Games. This teaches a certain survival mechanism in each of us (which I will also explain about more later). Learning this new state of mind and the resulting chemistry produced by it, is a good thing and not something that threatens your survival.

It is also important to constantly challenge your mind with any of the exercises that you learn, and to invent new exercises. I even secretly play some of my mind training games through lighthearted banter in my normal everyday life, while interacting with people who are taking my coffee order, working in restaurants or wherever I socialize, just to keep myself in practice.

WHY DO WE TEND TO RESIST IMPROVING OUR MINDS?

Earlier I talked about the effort it requires, as in going to work out in the gym, and most people don't want to work out in the gym, let alone working out with their minds. Yes, it does take effort to memorize things, but it requires a whole different order of effort to stretch your brain's capacity and speed.

The other tricky part is that there are two aspects involved: the physiological and the psychological. They can be looked at independently as well as through their interconnectedness. You have to also understand that we are not just a one-brain being, but a multi-brain being. (You can learn more about that in Peter Ouspensky's book entitled, *The Psychology of Man's Possible Evolution.*) To make things more complex, these multiple brains each have a different agenda and, in most cases, each brain does not know the others exist. Yet somehow we figure out how to walk around looking and acting as if we are one cohesive package.

The brain games in this book can help you to expand your master brain and deal with your multiple personalities and desires with fun and humor. It will get you in conscious contact with your mind's eye.

You can develop a master personality that will rule over all the other personalities in you. You will be able to see and deal with your contradictions better, reducing negative emotions and be able to make fun of yourself with more self confidence.

WHAT IS FORMATORY THINKING?

I briefly mentioned the term Formatory Thinking before so here are some examples of Formatory Thinking?

It is the: shoulds, shouldn'ts, compliant thinking; either/or absolute extreme thinking, black or white, no shades-of-gray thinking, taking ideas on face value because a so-called expert told you it was so. "Join the crowd and get away from it all" thinking, peer-pressure thinking, rebellious thinking just for the sake of rebelling and knee-jerk reactions.

Formatory Thinking is mechanical stimulus response thinking. It is crowd thinking and is responsible for turning an assembly into a mob. It is *obedience to authority* thinking, like the Stanley Milgram's book and experiments in the 1950's. It is where you assign your responsibility to thinking for yourself to someone else or some entity other than yourself.

Formatory Thinking is how the masses are controlled.

For example:

Think about what happens on what is called Black Friday, the day after Thanksgiving. The corporations have set up phenomena where they give you the illusion of special deals for Christmas. People camp out, stand in line for hours and when the doors open they act like animals toward each other. They are completely mindless, and if you were to show them a video of how they had behaved, they would not believe that they did what they did.

Then, every year right after Christmas, another blind mass of people have to rush back to the stores to return and exchange things. If that was not enough, they return in January for even bigger sales at even lower process than the Christmas sales, and the madness continues.

This behavior prevails, year after year. This is Formatory Thinking at its worst. We are all being duped constantly and put under so many unnecessary, imaginary pressures all the time, from consumerism to political obligations. The end result is greed and selfish behavior on all levels. Then you have political groups that actually pride themselves for being stubborn, uneducated and narrow-minded.

Getting away from all of this is truly like unplugging from the matrix of society, as in the movie of the same name. People are so immersed in this matrix that you need to use the Jaws of Life to get their minds to open and make them want to release themselves from its grip.

WHY DOES THE FORMATORY MIND FORM?

We all have in us what is called an "essence." This is a soft, impressionable psychological body which receives the impressions of the world. It cannot speak nor do anything; it only feels. It is very vulnerable too. As we go through life, this soft body starts to take a beating. In order for it to survive, it needs some protection. This protection is called our personality.

There are two kinds of personalities; a mechanical False Personality and an intentional True Personality. A False Personality is a wall, but a True Personality is a door. The False personality will not let the impressions of the world into its essence, and it will not allow our minds and hearts to mature and grow, The True Personality can allow impressions. A True Personality can still protect, and be operable to letting in the impressions of the world, at the appropriate time, to allow ourselves and our minds and hearts to mature.

How does it form?

Let's say you are at lunch at your first day of school and your essence is enjoying eating a banana. Some kid comes over to you and says" You're weird. You eat bananas."

What happens? The next day, you may stop eating bananas, hide eating bananas, start eating apples, or if you want to be accepted in a group, you start making others feel bad for eating bananas. Something has changed, and your relationship to enjoying the banana, which is part of your true essential self, has become contorted in some way.

This new behavioral modification becomes a small part of a vast collection of reactions to harsh experiences that make up the False Personality. It also changes and / or forms a particular mind-set about most everything in our lives.

But let's change the circumstances with a True Personality:

The same kid comes up to you and says "You're weird." You respond by saying, "I know. What's your point?"

In this case, you protected your essence and yet are able to continue to freely experience it. You can now still enjoy eating bananas, and maybe develop new recipes involving bananas. You see, your mind can still progress and mature without the interruption of trying to fit in. In order to evolve, we must develop and mature our essence, allow it to properly feel, and transform hurt and suffering into something beautiful, humorous and/or profound. This can also help one avoid unregulated anger and adult temper tantrums.

The ordinary conditions of life happen so quickly sometimes that we cannot react in ways we wish we would have in more relaxed, thoughtful situations. However, through the specific Brain Games in this book, you will be shown how to speed up your brain so that you can become the calm eye of the storm amidst the complicated situations of life.

So now, when you are in the ordinary conditions of life, decision making and actions are more easily made from a greater perspective of yourself and the situation. It also trains you how to transform potentially hurtful situations into humor and to form a stronger True Personality.

GOING BEYOND FORMATORY THINKING?

For the effectiveness of this experiment, try to do each direction before reading the next one.

Let's try a simple mind experiment:

ONE- Imagine yourself traveling through space as fast as you can.

TWO- Now double that speed and imagine that for a while.

THREE- Now double it again.

OK, stop!

I said "imagine yourself traveling through space as fast as you possibly can" and you formed an imaginary picture of how fast is fast. Why? Because when I said double that speed, you could. When I said double it again, maybe some of you could or some of you could not. But, even if you couldn't, you still formed an imaginary picture; however, this time it was, "I can't imagine it any faster."

But there is always faster, since we live in an infinite paradigm. How do I know we live in an infinite paradigm? Because I can simply imagine that infinity exists. So how fast is fast? How small is small? How empty is empty? What is it that we think we can or cannot do in our lives? Think!

Maybe scientists keep discovering that the universe gets bigger and particles get smaller simply because someone imagined it was possible. Maybe you can think and do some things that you thought you could not.

Formatory Thinking can range from simple things such as being immersed in traditions to ways scientists think about certain things, until someone makes a breakthrough.

One example of how Formatory Thinking limits our perceptions is when scientists say that the speed of light is the fastest speed in the universe. First of all, it is more accurate to say that the speed of light is presently the fastest speed in the universe that we know of. But even that isn't true. These statements contradict themselves in spite of all of this.

How?

Well I may not know how to create complex mathematical formulas, but I do know how to put two and two together.

According to the "Big Bang Theory," in the first ten seconds or so, after the Big Bang, the universe expanded many light years across. So something must be faster than light if the universe expanded many light years across in ten seconds or so.

Not only that, they have discovered that the universe is speeding up. So if the initial bang was faster than light, then the present state of expansion over billions of years must be even faster now. Unless, after the big bang the universe slowed down for a cup of hot tea for a few billion years and then took off again.

If it is true that the universe started out expanding faster than the speed of light and has been accelerating ever since, and we are part of this acceleration, then we are all traveling faster than the speed of light already.

Here is another mind experiment:

Imagine being at a star one hundred light years away in our universe on your left side. Now travel in your mind to a star one hundred light years away on your right side. How long did it take to get there? I bet a lot faster than the speed of light, right? So you might say, well of course, it is your imagination. But how do you know if our imaginations are not part of another real dimension and that is the way we can get around in that dimension? Our imagination, in and of itself, is also part of the known universe, isn't it? In fact, Einstein would travel through the universe in his mind all the time.

Yet another thought:

There are estimated to be over a septillion stars in the known universe.

That's: 1,000,000,000,000,000,000,000,000 stars. This does not include planets, moons and other objects. Nor does it include other dimensions and the micro subatomic world. All of these things are vibrating and sending out waves of information for us to receive. This affects what thoughts can potentially come into our minds.

With all those astronomical odds of possibilities, it then stands to reason, using my 2 + 2 = 4 method, that anything we imagine or can possibly imagine is true somewhere. So if you imagine that there are ham sandwiches walking around on a needle's point, it is true somewhere. It is simply mathematical.

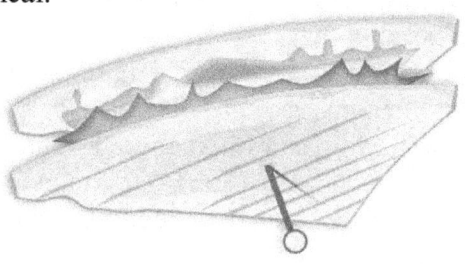

DEVELOPING THE SKILLS TO THINK ON HIGHER LEVELS

You can develop the skills to think on higher levels by learning how to think in new ways and constantly inventing new ways of thinking. You also can learn how to see yourself separate from your ideas and thoughts, and to observe them more objectively.

In order to develop the skills of thinking on a higher order, we first need to step back and re-evaluate almost everything we think we know and eliminate "self judgment."

Self judgment is the killer of anyone who wants to accomplish anything. Self judgment is learned and is not natural. It comes from social pressures, and the lack of competent education and educators.

For example:

Years ago, when my son was in the third grade, his teacher told the class to express themselves by drawing anything they wanted. My son, and the rest of the class, did so. The teacher actually graded their expressions and gave my son a C. When I found out about this, I was furious. I went to the teacher and asked her, "How can you judge anyone's, innocent self-expression objectively and who made you God?" She recognized my point of view, apologized and that was that. The event still irritates to this day.

Why?

It is because the whole system of grading both children and adults who are trying to learn is the worst system of education short of beatings. Grading is a mental and emotional beating, creating self-judgment, the death of inspiration and anything imaginative in people. It is a lazy, incompetent way to teach and is more about the failure of the teaching system than the students' ability to learn. It lacks insight and patience.

If you wake up the best opera singer, rouse them out of bed and ask them to immediately sing a beautiful note, what would you get? You would get something quite awful. If you were to base your opinion on their singing ability on the first fifty sounds that came out of them, it would be pretty bad. Eventually though, they would produce a beautiful note.

That is why I used to tell my students at the Academy of Art University to "Make the first thousand mistakes right away!" The difference between you and a professional is that they have made their thousand mistakes already and, as they make even more, they do not let mistakes defeat them. They are not afraid to start over.

Besides, what is a mistake anyway? Isn't it merely stepping from an expected reality into an unexpected one? The only real mistake is hesitating to adapt to the new situation. With the right training it is possible to adapt very quickly and cross over that mistake-threshold gracefully, thus turning what at one point could be considered a trip into a new dance step.

SO WHAT HAPPENED TO THE OPERA SINGER?

What happened to that opera singer was that she was warming up. Let me ask you this: If you are doing something creative for the first time, aren't you simply warming up for the first time? How can you judge yourself or others who are doing something in any creative endeavor for the first time? As a matter of fact, some of the most creative and innovative people make bigger and more extreme mistakes in the beginning of something they are learning, than people who become mediocre at something.

Why?

It is because they are testing the extreme limits of whatever they are attempting and, by doing so, will eventually be more innovative. This is different than those who are afraid to make a mistake, want to fit in and cannot even begin to be innovative. Another way of putting it is: "a complex computer program takes more time to load than a simple one."

WHAT IF I AM NOT A CREATIVE PERSON?

First of all, each of us has something we have done creatively in our lives. Everyone has had some moment of inspiration, even if it meant getting the idea to drive a different way to a particular destination. If you do not feel that you are a creative person, then you have had a cheated education. So let's get your creativity unleashed. Everyone has creative potential.

Second, simply wishing to be creative is a creative inspirational act. Now I'm not saying everyone can become a Leonardo da Vinci, but it doesn't matter; it is unnecessary to compare. You don't need another person's million moments of creativity to have an inspired experience. You simply need your own million moments of creative experiences for purposes of your own design.

HERE IS WHY EVERYONE HAS CREATIVE ENERGY

We all have creative energy, because we all have a sex drive. Sex energy is part of the creative life force in all of us. Another way to look at it is the opposite; that we have a life force in us and one vehicle to express it is through our sexuality. As we mature past puberty it is used for pro-creation or recreation. That is creativity on an instinctive level. Sex energy can also be transformed to create art, music or anything creative. That is also why beautiful environments are considered to be romantic. If you do not feel artistically creative, it is because no one has shown you how to transform sex energy in a creative direction. It is never too late to do so.

The thing that kept you from becoming creative as a child was self-judgment and it is self judgment now. All you need to do to be creative is to wish to be and start. The expression I like is:

"You don't need to be good to start. You just have to start to be good."

When you start, your brain has a chance to form more new neural pathways, and eventually the web of thoughts will start making connections, and your creativity will take off.

WHAT ABOUT THE MYSTICAL?

It is important first to define what *mystical* is.

If I had a smart phone and an internet connection one hundred years ago or more, it would be considered to be the most mystical device ever. It would be what technological dreams were made of. The device, or maybe even myself, would be considered to be either a super hero or god. If it was three hundred years ago, I might also be burned at the stake. Today we know about the technology of it, so it's not mystical.

There are some spiritual practices that are considered to be mystical because the psychological and physiological basis is unknown. But, if someone comes along and finds out what makes a particular practice or experience tick, scientifically, then there is nothing mystical about it anymore.

Why?

It is because the mystical is a place holder for knowledge and understanding. Once something is understood, then it is simply not mystical anymore.

IS THERE NO MYSTICAL?

There will always be something mystical, because discovering knowledge on one level can open up new questions on another level. However, if you find out the scientific workings about something and still persist in making it mystical, you are limiting your own ability to advance your mind, heart and soul.

We see this happening all the time in religious and/or spiritual cults when the leadership wants to maintain control and power over others for their own self-serving motives. Instead of teaching people how to be self-empowered, these leaders need to maintain a cloak of mystery and unattainable secrets to keep their followers in a lower, subservient place.

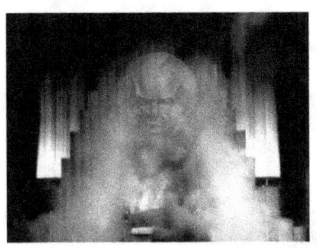

WHAT ABOUT ACQUIRING CERTAIN POWERS?

Years ago, I had a spiritual teacher that used to say, "Consciousness is a gift." Not knowing any better, I went along with it, until I woke up and realized something quite different. One day he again said, "Consciousness is a gift." This time I responded by saying, "No, consciousness is not a gift. Being dissatisfied with your relative consciousness is a gift. All the rest is conscious work, and, if you don't know how you got there and can't show others, clearly and plainly how to, then you are duped, and what you think you have is worthless and an illusion about consciousness." After that, I had to leave that group, because I had snatched the pebble from my teacher's hand.

If someone offers you a special power, and you do not know how it works, what is the real value of it? It would only end up corrupting you and your actions. Earned powers are the only guarantee for creating humility and restraint. We certainly see all kinds of people in charge that are corrupted by their powers and their control over others.

Lao Tzu said, "Controlling others requires force, controlling the self requires strength."

MULTI- PSYCHOLOGICAL BEINGS?

I have mentioned a few times how there is a part of us that doesn't want to pursue increasing our mental capacity because of fears, laziness, etc.? Well here is why:

We are not just a one brain being, but a mutibrained being. These brains exist for the most part for their own agenda and do not know or care about the existence of the other brains.

For example:

Simultaneously, one brain needs to eat pizza now; another brain needs to take a shower now another needs to make an important phone call now, etc. We see this dilemma happening in us all the time and we have to set priorities.

We actually have four basic brains, Instinctive, Moving, Emotional and Intellectual, each with three sub categories. For now, I will just talk about the four basic brains. Each brain has a different speed. The Intellectual brain is the slowest, next is the

Instinctive, next the Moving and the fastest brain is the Emotional brain.

This can be observed in the following example:

If someone is feeling angry at you, and is about to throw something at you, it is the Emotional brain that senses it first because it is the fastest. Then they throw it at you, and your Moving brain will attempt to get out of the way. Then your Instinctive brain pumps adrenaline, and your heart rate goes up. This all happens before the Intellectual brain has a chance to say, "Gee, he just threw something at me."

When we want to become more conscious and do some practices, like meditation for example, we involve a higher Emotional brain endeavor accompanied by the Intellectual brain. Now even though the Intellectual brain is the slowest, it has time before an actual experience to figure out what you want to do in advance. The Instinctive brain, on the other hand, will not know what is going to happen until it does happen, so even though it is faster than the Intellectual brain, it does not know about planning. It only knows now. Besides, the whole experience is being driven by the Emotional brain.

When you start to have this conscious experience, a different chemistry is produced in the body, not the least of which is the pineal gland that sends out melatonin which acts as an endocrine hormone. There is also the factor of the unknown from a new situation that activates the adrenals (the fight-or-flight mechanism) of the Instinctive brain. In such situations, the Instinctive brain, sensing a sudden unknown chemistry unaccompanied with the fear of the unknown, produces what is called a *buffer*.

Buffers can range from an imaginary itch to a mental distraction to negative emotions. This is primarily what keeps us from staying on track when pursuing something out of our normal patterns. In the case of meditation, it will create distracting thoughts or even sleep.

With humor as a learning tool, I introduce an intentional buffer. It is accompanied by a little shot of endorphins. It also allows the truth and the ability to see one's contradiction from a distance; thus the possibility of change. In the past, there was a conscious School of Jesters formed in the royal courts. The Jesters knew about using humor as a tool, and used it to influence their rulers without getting their heads cut off.

So the first thing that you do is to learn how to cleanse your magnetic field. This makes you open to doing the second thing, which is channeling.

MORPHIC FIELDS AND CHANNELING

In 1991 Dr. Rupert Sheldrake, an English biologist, started talking about Morphic Fields. The basic premise is that plants, animals and even humans can, pick up and respond to the same wavelengths of ideas, events, emotions, etc., simultaneously; in other words a collective subliminal learning, irrespective of location. I did not know it, nor did I have the terminology for it at the time, but it turns out that, along with Sheldrake's characterization of Morphic fields, I was experimenting with techniques on how we can personally access what I call creative energy fields with each other all over the planet. As you read more about Morphic Fields, you will see how poetically ironic this is.

Since there is so much work that has already been done and still is being done in defining Morphic Fields, my contribution is to help to identify more of them and show people how to access and experience them for themselves.

Morphic Resonance is the ability to tune into different kinds of wavelengths or cosmic magnetic Fields. These fields are resonating around our planet all the time. They are responsible for a wide range of phenomena, including how schools of fish or flocks of birds know how to stay together and move simultaneously, and how humans visualize the same ideas at the same time whether they are a foot away or half a world apart.

It was first observed in the UK in the 1950's, when milk was still being delivered to your door in glass bottles with a little cardboard seal inserted in the top. The birds would try to pry open the caps to get to the cream at the top but couldn't. One day, while an ornithologist in the UK was talking on the phone to a colleague in Germany, he observed for the first time a bird finally being able to pry open the milk bottle seal. He mentioned it to his German friend who told him that he had observed the same thing happening about an hour earlier for the first time too. The birds got the same message at the same time. They were tuned into the same wavelength.

Since then, there have been numerous studies and experiments conducted on this subject that confirmed that this is happening all the time. In a recent study in the US utilizing a specially designed computer program, which was able to learn how to analyze and relate certain brain patterns to human thoughts, was able to register certain human responses. Researchers could see a person's reaction and could anticipate what would happen up to six seconds before it happened. In other words there is empirical proof that it is humanly possible to anticipate the future at least up to six seconds.

Here is some more evidence:

René Descartes discovered analytic geometry while Sir Isaac Newton and Gottfried Wilhelm von Leibniz discovered calculus. The two subjects embody the same basic mathematical principles. René Descartes did not know of Sir Isaac Newton and Gottfried Wilhelm von Leibniz and vice versa, yet they discovered these respective mathematical principles approximately at the same time.

The US patent office frequently gets similar requests for patents within hours of each other.

You must also ask yourself, why is it that once a year a bunch of fashion industry professionals get the same or similar ideas for fashion and color, year after year? The reason for this is because of magnetic Morphic Fields.

Since I have been experiencing Holographic Thinking and teaching others, we have all had experiences with Morphic Resonance. In fact, while both observing and performing in the mind training games, not only do the performers have the experience but anyone just observing does too.

Here is a very direct experience you can all relate to:

When we talk to each other, we make *statements*, but what we really are trying to accomplish is to communicate a common state of mind or *states-of-mind-meant*.

This is all about channeling Morphic Fields and we do it all the time when we ask, "Do you know what I mean?"

The value of this is the understanding that there are whole worlds of sub-textual experiences going on during our so-called ordinary lives. When you are able to tap into the Holographic Thinking process and learn to let the Inner mind do its work, all kinds of additional benefits occur.

I suspect Einstein knew about this, if not by some defined principles as I am elucidating, but by his own method of tapping into the knowledge of the universe. He certainly did visualize.

Now, whether a person is aware of this or not, doesn't change the real effects of it. We all respond to these influences continually and they affect not only our daily lives but, on some greater scale, all of humanity.

HOW TO CHANNEL

There is one very important factor in channeling: getting the ego out of the way. This means eliminating self-judgment. Self-judgment is the major obstacle for just about anything we want to do. It is also connected to vanity.

Vanity is lying in wait, looking for any chance to take credit for even selfless acts. As is said in Ecclesiastes; *vanity of vanities all is vanity*. Vanity can be very clever and insidious. The most amazing performance of vanity is acting humble. Accepting we are vain and moving on is the better policy.

To channel you need to get yourself out of the way. This can be done through Holographic Thinking. Not just any Holographic Thinking either, but Holographic Thinking with a different twist to it. The different twist is that you are inspired.

To begin to channel:

To begin to channel on your own and I say *to begin*, because there are many ways to channel after you get the basic idea down, you need to find a quiet space, state of mind, or find something that represents what you want to channel and endow it. *Endowing* means that you give it credibility for the focus of whatever you are trying to channel. Some calming music or nature sounds can also help. This is a slower way to learn how to channel than the group exercises, but it still possible, especially if you are by yourself and have no other choice.

Stop thoughts about everything except for the thought of what you want to channel. Just do a basic meditation of observing your breath, all the while holding a picture in your mind of the endowed object or thought in the back of your mind.

Now follow the steam of ideas that flow through your mind, record them in some way, but never judge them. "The road to great ideas is paved by idiotic ones."

Do this for about five minutes or however long your mind keeps coming out with ideas. Then forget about it and go about your business for another day or two. Go back and review your previous ideas and see which ideas are connected.

If you do not get all of the results by then, repeat the process another day and accumulate results. You might be surprised to find that your vision is channeled right away and may even take you in a completely different direction than you expected.

Now here are a few things to keep in mind:

First, as mentioned, the results you are seeking may be very different than what you expected.

Second, your results may be part of a continuum, and you may just get partial results and need to continue.

Third, it simply may not be time for the results you are looking for, so simply repeat the process every so often.

Fourth, an idea may evolve over time and you may need to channel it many times, even though you have initial results.

For example:

Anytime someone asks me a question about anything, I revisit and think about whatever subject they are asking about and formulate a new unique answer to that question. If someone asks me how I feel about something, like this very subject of channeling, I will look at it fresh and find a new way to describe how I see and feel about it in that moment.

It is a bit more difficult to recognize results on your own, than in a group improv situation where you are in the moment and are pressured to respond without thinking. But you can set up personal mental challenges to respond immediately if you are being honest with yourself.

This is the faster way for results. You just express a whole bunch of things that pop out of your head, write them down in a word or two, continue to find more ideas and, when you have maybe ten of them, then take a break. When you come back, re-evaluate them, maybe combine or see what other related ideas come as a result.

Of course, when you are inspired, you are tuned in to something, and the whole picture unfolds before your very eyes.

Remember, just because you channeled one truly inspired idea, does not mean you cannot channel more. This is what separates a typical "run of the mill" channeler, from a more objective one.

WHAT EVOKES HOLOGRAPHIC THINKING?

Holographic Thinking is a three dimensional experience in thinking. It requires the use of all of your brain's facilities at the same time. I usually say the left and right brain, but there are other parts that have to participate too.

What activities produce Holographic Thinking?

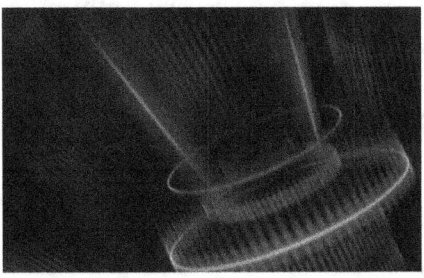

Holographic Thinking is any activity that requires you to both have a structure and to be creative, and respond spontaneously within that structure. When you are naturally inspired, you experience the properties of Holographic Thinking, and you are channeling.

Examples:

Perspective Drawing - You need to work within a blend of structured vanishing points and visualization. This is what made the Renaissance such a creative explosive time. More painting per capita was done in that time than ever before and rivals the amount of artwork even being produced today. Perspective drawing is one of the tools that Leonardo da Vinci used to think in new ways.

Creating Mathematical Formulas – This requires both technical skills, through the holding in your mind of several concepts in three dimensions, and visualization. Einstein would do this as he actually visualized astrophysical principles.

Martial Arts – Each form of martial arts has "Katas," a practice of form or dance. When sparring, you need to be creative within the context of the form of Katas. Balancing the form in the context of actual combat, makes your brain access more of itself.

Improvisation- In improvisation you need to play within the rules of a game, at least to start, and then visualize and perform within that framework. Improv is the martial arts of the brain. It speeds up your mind, beyond what you think you can do.

Playing a Musical Instrument- Playing an instrument, like the piano, violin, drums or guitar, where you use your hands along with other body parts, doing different tasks, will evoke Holographic Thinking.

Peripheral Vision- When engaging in peripheral vision you must look and sense almost 360 degrees around you. Not just that, but engage in peripheral hearing, the ability to hear distant sounds near and far. In both cases it widens your perceptions and creates new neural pathways seeing more than one thing at the same time.

Out of Patterns- By using the weaker sides of your body to do the mechanical tasks that the stronger parts of your body normally do, you can get things out of patterns. If you routinely use your right hand to open something, instead use your left hand. This will also stimulate thinking differently. Leonardo da Vinci was ambidextrous and, on occasion, wrote backwards. This was part of his self-training.

As a matter of fact, many times, reversing little expressions can bring new insight.

For example:

People say, "Great minds think alike." Instead say; "Great minds like to think."

Instead of thinking "out of the box," how about doing some actual thinking "in the box."

Instead of "Be prepared," what we say in improv theater is, "Don't be prepared."

Think about what the true meaning of expressions are and then reverse them. Sometimes the opposite might be truer.

Free-Form Dancing - Dancing free-form, making up moves as you go along, is a physical way to initiate Holographic Thinking. There is a wordless intelligence in the body that is set free by improvisational dancing. Personally, all the ideas from my first book came to the surface while I was dancing many years ago.

Rock Climbing- Rock climbing forces you to be very creative and spontaneous in very intense conditions. It uses the same mechanism as dancing and improv.

Looking Exercise- As you look around the room, you keep your eyes moving before your brain can form a name associated with any object. This is a way to stop your thoughts. By stopping mundane thoughts, very important thoughts will involuntarily force their way into your consciousness.

Divided Attention - Become aware of the world outside of yourself, as well as the inside world of your reactions.

Here is the special twist, which makes the whole thing a bit easier in a certain way. You must separate and be the "observer" of the outside world and your reactionary inside world. A little trick I use is to ask myself:

"Am I my eyes or that which is looking out of my eyes?"

"Holographic Thinking" requires you to be separate and observe the whole process, without comment. You will come to see yourself as an intermediary of the process that is carrying out your channeling duties.

You will learn how to trust that there is an Inner Mind that works all on its own, and knows how to channel what you need to do. This has been demonstrated time and time again in my brain training classes. In improv, it is where the performer goes on the stage to change or add something to a particular scene, not because they have an idea of how to do so, but because the scene needs to be changed.

I tell the trainees not to have any ideas until they get into position. When they get on the stage and in position, they are amazed at what comes out all on its own. There is an Inner Working Mind that knows what to do, and it rises to the occasion.

Not So Complicated:

Does this sound complicated or impossible? Well actually not; this happens all the time when we are inspired.

When you are inspired, what you consider to be "you" is separate and observing what your body, heart and mind are doing, but not taking claim to it. The moment you do take claim, you lose the inspiration. When it is all over, you are as amazed at what you have done as any other outside observer. In a way, more so because it is shocking to have this experience and the longer you have those kinds of inspirational experiences, the more shocking it becomes. This is because you suddenly feel like some kind of puppet in a play.

There are also some pitfalls too, because our vanity is right there looking to take claim. Many great people have failed just on the verge of success because of this mechanism of vanity.

Being separate from what you are observing is the "Inner Body" experience. With all of those different ways of activating Holographic Thinking, I have found the fastest way to becoming more proficient at it is through using improvisation acting games with others. Why? It is because you get to laugh, have fun, and have some peer pressure in good spirit. This is more effective than being on your own.

The three most important things about improv are: you have to be in the moment, be in the moment and be in the moment. No cheating, just pure experience.

Also, using humor and peer pressure, enables you to spend enough flight time in that altered state of consciousness. The instinctive part, our survival mechanism, can learn the new chemistry and that the new experience of being in this higher state is a good thing. You want to get that Instinctive brain to work with you not against you.

POWER SHARING

Too many times, people who reach a certain level of achievement fall into the trap of feeling that their method is the only way and, unless you have gone through their learning process, you don't have valid ideas. To work with others requires knowing how to power share. Power sharing involves validating others' ideas whether they are consciously experienced or not, professional or not, talented or not.

There is so much information in the marketplace on becoming self-empowered. Becoming self empowered means a lot of time, effort and sacrificing. It also means developing a certain amount of will and concentration. In power sharing, you have to give up your imaginary picture of needing to control, and share the control with another person in order to learn, consider their ideas and perceptions.

The key thought is this:

If what you have gained through the process of self-empowerment is real, then you cannot lose it; so giving it over to someone else for a moment or two, should not make a difference. Once you gain a certain level of self-empowerment and self confidence, you will be constantly challenged and in many ways broken down to your core, and have to rebuild yourself with what you know for sure and what you can depend on.

It is actually part of the law of nature, where animals challenge the dominant leader. In this case however, instead of meeting the challenge head on in conflict or running away in fear, power sharing takes the energy and redirects it for the benefit of all involved.

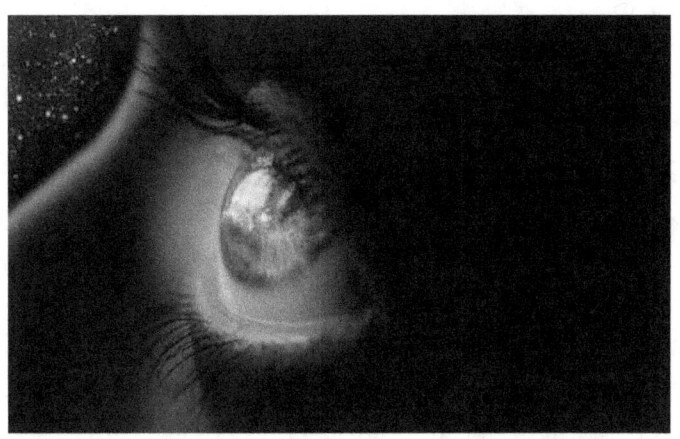

STIMULATING IMAGINATION

If I were to ask you to make up a story, RIGHT NOW, one that had never been a story before; what would your reaction be?

Would you hesitate and need to think about it first?

But if I asked you to visualize the first images that pop into your head in response to the following questions, let's see what happens:

Imagine you are standing in some imaginary place, Where is it?

Who is standing next to you?

They have something in their hand. They hand it to you. What is it?

What do they say to you as they hand it to you?

And you say what in response?

Suddenly something flies by. What is it?

At that point you decide to do what?

Your response here might be quite different than just having to make up a whole story on the spot. You can fill in the blanks to those questions or others like it all day. You could start over repeatedly and continue to come up with new images. At this rate you could write numerous books without skipping a beat if you had enough questions to visualize the answers to. In fact:

"It's not a lack of answers that keep us from making new discoveries. It's a lack of questions."

POSITIVE ENVIRONMENT

It is also vital to know how to develop ideas without short-circuiting them. Many people have good ideas but, they cannot develop them beyond the idea stage. We have learned patterns of behavior that sabotage our ideas and keep them from going anywhere. These behavior patterns also set up situations that can keep others within our influence from developing their ideas.

We need to know how to create a positive atmosphere conducive to the development of the imagination of all those around us. Anyone who has worked within a well-functioning team knows that one productive imagination can feed many imaginations. When all the team members' imaginations work together, the possibilities are unlimited. Many of us also know what it is like to be creatively squelched by a restricted work environment.

Positive Attitude / Joyful Creation:

Take the time to see a clear picture of yourself envisioning what you want to create. Have a positive image of yourself, and do not let go of it. If you lose this positive image of yourself envisioning, writing or thinking... stop. Then refocus on the image and the good feelings you have about yourself.

It is important to have those good, enjoyable feelings when we create, because with those feelings almost anything is possible. We can also see and perceive things that don't happen to us when we have neutral, indifferent, pressured, stressed or negative feelings.

It's not the ability to create and be original you don't have that matters; it's the desire to be creative and original that you do have that counts!

This is what can prime the pump for inspiration.

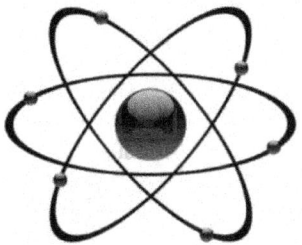

UNLIMITED CREATIVITY

In our lifetime each of us has been given a certain measure of creative energy. You could describe it as something akin to human nuclear fuel or talent. What we do with this fuel or talent makes all the difference. How much is actually there is difficult to quantify, and it varies from individual to individual. However, one thing is obvious: when creativity exists in vast quantities, there is nothing that can keep it from expressing itself.

We have many examples of this throughout history where musicians, painters, inventors and scientists lived in oppressive situations and still managed to produce, more than if they had not had those restrictions. An example of this is a 1993 survey of Russian artists, which revealed that the artists were producing less than when they were rebelling against the restrictive Soviet Union.

It is hard for us to see ourselves in relation to how much creative energy we have because we are so subjective about it.

When we feel creative, we think it's never going to end. And when we don't feel creative, we think it's never going to return.

CREATIVE BALANCE

We can acquire an unlimited amount of creative energy by tapping directly into our natural reactions and re-routing them in a specific direction of our choice. In order to do this we need to understand our natural Inner Mind and what our own individual natural reactions are. In turn, we have to be true to these natural reactions.

By reaching a creative balance between our instincts, movements, intellect, emotions and sexuality, we can experience our natural reactions more clearly. Each of the elements in us has its own agenda and needs, which are quite often, independent of each other. It is worthwhile to understand and develop each part's unique creative intelligence. If balance can be attained, then it can sustain us, keep our creativity vital and bridge creative blocks.

If we can define what each element is in ourselves, we can go down the checklist and know which present governing faculty in us at any given moment wishes to be expressed. Balance between all of these different entities within us can be achieved by nourishing or exercising each part regularly.

Denying any one of these elements for too long tends to interfere and throw us off balance. It's as if we have a great multivitamin but we are missing a certain trace mineral in our diets; even though we only need a little bit of it, when we do not get it over a long period of time, it can become the most important thing in our lives. It can dominate all that we do. We may even sacrifice our multivitamin to get it.

A great deal of self-expression can also be about depicting, in some form, what the missing elements are in our lives. Through self-expression, we can see what is needed and try to provide it for ourselves. This does not mean that we can provide some things over night either, although it would be nice if life were so simple. Just remember to not be judgmental about your needs or the needs of others.

The Brain Games provided in this book can help you find this balance, because they make you use all of your senses.

NATURAL REACTIONS AND CREATIVITY

The ability to respond "naturally" to a situation takes time and practice and people have to work on it every day. Why? Because, through their False Personalities, people have become so jaded and insulated from their own natural responses and have bought into their programming from childhood, in schools, through media and institutions. Therefore, getting in touch with our core selves requires the task of deprogramming from this lifelong conditioning.

When we eventually get in touch with our core selves by understanding those natural reactions, it leads us to perceiving the world around us in an original way. This is very empowering. Our ability to express our real selves can be disarming to other people. Their response to us can range from empathy and moving their own spirit, to criticism and extreme fear. Most people are not able to express themselves and their real needs, and they secretly wish they could.

The way to create more meaning and depth in our creativity is to utilize in some way, our natural reactions and perceptions. It is these perceptions that lead us to originality. Our natural perceptions (from the Inner Mind) can be as unique as snowflakes.

When we find ourselves in a situation that requires us to react very quickly, we are more prone to react naturally without some affectation of our personalities and self-judgment getting in the way.

Also, just because we react with natural reactions does not mean we have come to the final destination of our creative development. It means that we can now see clearly those things that we may want to modify for a specific situation and move our creative development forward.

114

For example:

In one of my Brain Games, I direct the participants to accept whatever idea or object is presented to them and use it positively in their response that they are making up together. I use the example of handing someone a handful of horse manure. The natural reaction is to possibly say, "No, keep it yourself." Instead, I direct them to react by saying something like, "Thank you. I needed that for my collection." Now it becomes funny.

What transpires here is, first, they have to become aware of their natural reaction to reject the manure. Then they can gain more control and turn the situation around by intentionally acting out in a different way. People will see how this reaction is unusual. That is what makes it funny and unique. Just having natural reactions isn't enough sometimes, but it is where we have to start over, again and again.

CREATIVE MOVEMENT

A rudimentary way to develop our natural reactions, free of self-judgment, is through free-flowing movement. I have found that regardless of any creative endeavor, there is an inherent knowledge, without words, that the body has. If we learn to tap into this, we can have a greater strength, flow and breadth to our creativity.

I have often used free form, improvisational dancing to clear my mind. I can allow myself to dance and move freely, warming up my body in its own way and at its own pace. In an evening of dance, I can shuck off practically all the weight of responsibilities and tensions that I carry around, either real or imaginary, and get down to my basic relaxed self. When in this state of release of mind and body, amazing creative thoughts come out. I keep a small notepad handy so I can record these ideas for later use.

Dancing has been a major way that practically all cultures have cleansed and renewed themselves throughout recorded history. It is interesting to see how in our modern-day environment most people, especially as they get older, have practically lost track of this vital tool and have even begun to fear it. This is an indication of being close-minded, mechanical and uncreative. Using free-form dance can get you back to your true nature!

HUMOR AND CREATIVITY

Tremendous obstacles are placed in the way of our creativity; one of the main ones is negative emotions. They can defeat us and deny us the ability to see life objectively. Negative emotions can take many forms and, at times, even fool us into thinking that an attitude is not negative.

For example:

One might think of indifference as a neutral emotion. In fact, indifference has a slightly negative charge to it. The types of emotions to have when being creative are neutral, but slightly positive. In other words you have to have some caring for what you are doing. This is a hard balance to achieve since we do not want to have so much caring we get too immersed and lose our sense of being the observer. We need to have just the right amount of care to proceed, but not so much that our ability to change direction cannot be achieved. This is where humor can play a vital role in creativity.

Humor can bridge the resistance to change and, thus, help greatly to compensate for all the missing or deficient elements in ourselves. It can help us be innovative, but not be consumed by our specific endeavor. Humor is the great transformer. It can take a seemingly hopeless situation and, in a matter of seconds, change it to a wholly different dimension.

It can help us see ourselves and do something about it. It can help us maintain perspective on what we are doing, and keep us from taking ourselves too seriously and getting lost in self-indulgence. It can be just the push we need to be more flexible, to change something or some idea that holds us back.

It is precisely humor and whimsy that are the main tools that accelerate the creative and learning process.

Einstein was known for his sense of humor, and Leonardo even wrote jokes in his note books.

THINKING IN A NEW WAY

Thinking in a new way is not as obvious as one might expect. Usually we find ourselves taking new ideas and trying to fit them into our old ways of thinking, and people don't even know they are thinking in their typical way, because they don't yet comprehend what thinking differently actually means.

Looking at a particular idea with a new or different perspective takes either unusual experiences or special training. In order to learn to think in a new way, we need a taste of that experience. This can provoke a desire to want more special training and understanding of how it all works, so we can integrate it.

If we see ourselves as beginners, we allow ourselves to become an unshaped piece of clay for the world to make its current impression on us. In order to illustrate the value of being fresh and unique, I use as an example the story of The Master Chicken Feeder.

> Once upon a time, there was a Master Chicken Feeder who knew everything you could know about feeding chickens. People would come to him from miles around for advice. He had an apprentice working for him, trying to learn everything he could from the Master so that he, too, someday could become a Master Chicken Feeder.

One day, while the Master Chicken Feeder went to the fields to collect more chicken feed, the Village Idiot came into the chicken house and watched the apprentice feeding the chickens. Suddenly the Village Idiot said to the apprentice, "You shouldn't feed the chickens like that!" And he started to grab the feed bag from the apprentice.

The apprentice quickly pulled the feed bag out of the Idiot's hand and said, "Don't tell me how to feed chickens. I am learning how to feed chickens from the Master Chicken Feeder!" At that moment the Master arrived back from the fields and started to feed the chickens.

The Village Idiot turned to the Master, this time, "You shouldn't feed chickens like that. You should do it this way!" With that he started to grab the feed bag. Instead of snatching the bag out of his reach, the Master handed the Idiot the feed bag and watched intently how the Idiot fed the chickens. After a few minutes, the Idiot handed the Master back the feed bag, and the Master said, "Thank you, I didn't know you could feed chickens that way."

The moral of the story is:

"An amateur thinks they can only learn from a master, but a master can learn from everything, even an idiot."

FALSE SOCIAL-MORAL MOTIVATIONAL THEORY

Somewhere along the line of modern social-moral ideology, someone got the idea that the only way a person can be motivated is through struggle. If a person was not having to struggle to survive and acting stressed and somewhat negative, they were not really working. This idea is ridiculous, outdated and is the result of Formatory Thinking.

Curiosity and the need for understanding can be motivation themselves. A child's wonderment about the world around them is very strong and self-motivating. They have drive and desire to succeed without being driven by survival. When a child, at an early age, is given a healthy dose of creative encouragement added to their wonderment, they can develop good self esteem, wanting to learn and to do something productive.

In turn, they can be creatively motivated on their own throughout the rest of their lives. If you look closely at the lives of most people, whether they were encouraged to be creative or not, there is something that they find in their lives that is creative. When I think of this particular idea of creative motivation, a cartoon from the satirical cartoonist Gary Larson comes to mind:

The cartoon shows a man sitting in his easy chair at home reading the newspaper. Outside the window you can see a steamroller parked in the driveway. You can tell from this, that what he does for a living is drive that steamroller. The humorous part was on his walls: his art was flattened and framed road kill.

Each person, on their own and to their own degree, has a natural desire to be creative in the same way each person has their own unique desire for sex. Somehow it is going to be taken care of. This does not mean that there will not be struggles that occur in each of our lives. These struggles can be useful and even necessary. But it is not our job to create obstacles for other people, rather to create opportunities. It is nature's job to provide these obstacles, not other humans.

Instead of unemployment agencies encouraging us to find jobs where our creativity is usually stifled, there should be "self-employment agencies" educating us on how to create jobs, businesses and expand our lives and the lives of others. The real creative struggle of life is to struggle against mediocrity. That in itself is challenge enough.

The greatest gift to humans is that there are some that are always dissatisfied with whatever amount of knowledge they have and continually want more.

DIRECTED LEARNING

I am sure that we have all had the same experience:

We have a hard time getting up early when we have to go to work or school, no matter how early we went to bed. Then the weekend comes or we are on vacation and amazingly, get up early in the morning when we do not have to, even if we were up late the night before.

Another experience every parent has gone through is this:

Your child tells you that they are tired, that they cannot do something, or that they cannot walk another step. The next thing you know, they see a friend and they start playing and running around as if they had just swallowed a hornet's nest.

Or how about this:

You're tired and exhausted; you just sat down after a hard day's work, and you get a phone call from someone who says, "Your great uncle Louie, whom you have never met has just passed away and left you a million dollars. But he stated in his will that the only way you can have it is if you drive across the country right now and get it." You sure would get a tremendous burst of energy, wouldn't you?

All three of these scenarios are examples of the power of inspiration. With the provocation of enough inspiration we could learn to do anything. My son could sit still for hours and concentrate without any pause on his video game. The amount of energy, intricate maneuvers and problem solving that went into his playing that game is probably enough to solve the world's energy problem.

If we have the capabilities of such energy and focus, then why does traditional education make so many children feel like throwing up before they go to school in the morning?

It's because traditional educational practices treat children like Learning Automatons. They work with a teaching curve model that programs mediocrity. The actual learning curve is entirely different.

Here is the typical teaching curve:

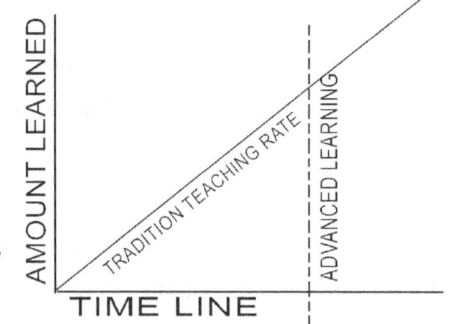

This line presupposes that children learn in a straight line. This process throws many subjects at the children on a constant basis. It never really allows them enough time to master any particular thing, unless they are naturally gifted and interested in a particular area. It forces subjects and material down the children's throats before they are ready. It does not tap into their inspiration. It does not give them the sense of accomplishment and self-confidence to want to concentrate and learn. There

125

is no time to spend on letting the children completely grasp one idea before more information and/or tests pressure them and force them to stumble.

The students have to hit the ground running, and many significant elements of the basic understanding of learning are lost. They are reduced to the memorization of facts and figures, and the students with the best memories win. They really never learn how to learn to critically think. The children that have good memorization skills follow the teaching curve, but later their learning rate falls off to almost nothing.

This is the actual learning curve of this teaching method:

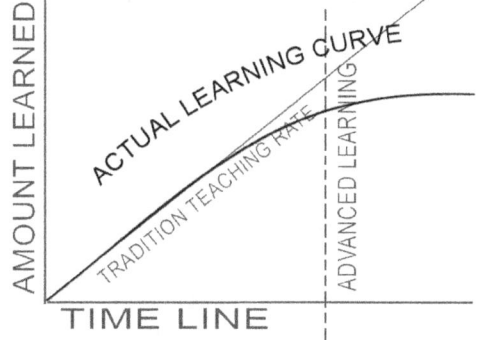

Think about how adults learn something that they really desire and want to learn later in life, with no pressure, and not for a grade.

First of all, they don't necessarily take six subjects at a time. They might stop the instructor more often to ask more questions. If there are younger adults in the class, they might feel that the class is being slowed down by the older adults. But as the class

126

progresses, the older adults seem to leap past the younger students in their basic understanding of the particular subject. This is because they are learning with inspiration and, therefore, they want to thoroughly understand a subject.

Since they have more experience in life in general, the information they take-in is being related to a broader range of experiences. This takes more time, but the end result is that when they finally understand the information, they can relate it to more things and end up with a broader understanding of that particular subject.

Here is the learning curve based on inspiration:

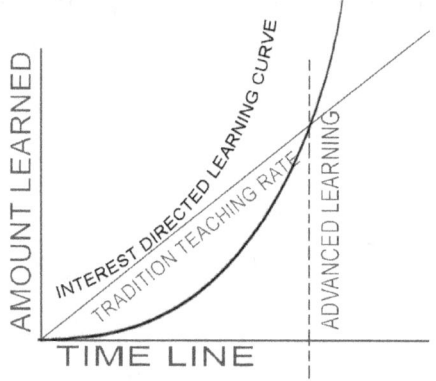

You will see that in the beginning it appears slow, but then it takes off exponentially. By teaching children with more understanding of their individualized complexities, we can direct the students toward their natural interests and let them experience the growth of their self confidence.

Everything is connected. If you follow through with any subject matter far enough, you will eventually get to all the other subjects. For example:

A child wants to learn about space; so he sees a video. Then he wants to know how the moon revolves around the earth. He is shown experiments in physics about gravity and centrifugal force. At that point, you might introduce the fact that you can predict certain events using mathematics.

Maybe the child wants to get some information from NASA. You help him write a letter; you show him what is important about communication, writing and spelling, etc. This is just a small example of the "connectedness" of things, and, all the while, the information is being dispensed using the child's inspiration.

This does not mean that learning does not include some struggle and self-discipline. With the "connectedness" of things, we have a greater chance of accomplishment regarding the child's success. With the self confidence each child achieves, we can inspire them to struggle and conquer any new topic.

Whenever possible, it is better to teach a student how to access and develop their own creative ideas, not those of the teacher. Teachers all too often fall into patterns of teaching and assigning the same projects over and over. It is better to let students be driven by their own interests because they will learn more.

For example:

I asked students in my conceptual design classes why they were in design school. They would say things like they wanted to design a museum, a new kind of homeless shelter, their own ultimate house, etc.

I would then make that their first assignment. Instead of battling for their interest on a project I would assign, I had a captive audience. Now I could concentrate on helping them dig deep into themselves. The results were very revealing. The students soaked up just about everything I would say and felt so satisfied with their projects that they were completely ready to take on any project that I would make up next. One student, who designed an archeology museum, was so satisfied with her project that she changed her major, because she decided that she really wanted to become an archeologist instead.

How many times have we sought something, maybe for years, and finally attained it, only to find out that it really wasn't what we wanted after all. Wouldn't it be great if our teachers could help us to find our real vocations by giving us the opportunity to experience our creative fantasies right away? Some people struggle all their lives wanting to create something and never do. The student needs to be taught how to pursue his or her dreams.

ALL LEARNING IS CONNECTED

Before we can learn to do many things well, we first have to learn how to do one thing well. This is because the same learning elements are involved in all learning endeavors. There is always a point of struggle and the need for perseverance, and a point of resolution and elation. Then there is a point of dissatisfaction and the need to struggle again. By seeing ourselves succeed at something after the struggle, we can begin see that the reason we are struggling is because we are forming new neural pathways and with rest, the necessary connections will be made. Then you will be able to proceed further.

Once you understand this process, you will be able to learn anything, to anticipate some difficulties, but not to give up. By anticipating some difficulties and know that perseverance and rest will eventually make you successful, you will actually advance faster at learning because you will not be wasting time, blaming yourself for failure and self judgment.

Almost anything, no matter how difficult to learn in the beginning, eventually becomes easier as perseverance furthers. Knowing how this process works enables you to learn many things, not just generally, but in a thorough way.

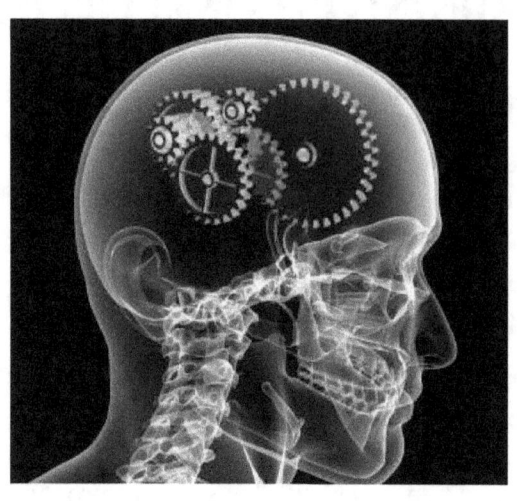

INNER AUTOMATIC PROBLEM SOLVING MIND (IAPSM)

Have you ever had the experience of trying to solve something? You struggle and struggle and you just don't get it. You give up, walk away and, a few hours or days later, *BOING!* You get it, you figure it out, and you didn't even want to think about it anymore. This demonstrates that there is something in us that is still working to solve problems even when we aren't consciously aware of it. We have in us a powerful decision-making and creative mechanism. What is this faculty in us and can we allow this faculty to be present more frequently?

Although we are channeling wavelengths, we still have a mechanism that interprets what the wavelengths are transmitting automatically. This faculty is the "Inner Automatic Problem Solving Mind" (IAPSM). We have constant surface mind chatter going on in our heads. The IAPSM is deeper and separate from this chatter. Everyone experiences IAPSM to one degree or another more commonly than you might expect.

This faculty is really nothing. I mean really nothing: a vacuum. Leonardo da Vinci said, "The soul is like a vacuum, and the main property of a vacuum is that everything wants to fill it." If we can imagine our IAPSM to be like a vacuum, we can access many ideas that are attracted to the intentional vacuum of thought we produce.

A good mind exercise I do frequently for brainstorming is the No Thoughts exercise. This is how it works:

Find a quiet place with few distractions. Think about nothing. Don't dwell on any subject, no matter how enticing. Thoughts will try to enter the mind at the front door. Instead of fighting the ideas from entering, simply let them out the back door.

Keep up this process for as long as you can. Practice it once a day, preferably at the same time every day in order to keep up the discipline, or whenever you need to develop an idea. You will find that, at first, it is easy to let the thoughts out the back door. Then a very interesting thought comes along, and you might find yourself slowly escorting it out the back door.

Don't let that thought divert you!

If you can persist long enough, you will soon have some great realization and probably find yourself sailing off into creative imagination. Write down the ideas. Then resume with the mind exercise for as long as you can. You will soon see the results of the Inner Mind.

This is only one way to access the IAPSM, but there are many ways. The IAPSM is the core of all our superior thought calculations; it is an endless reservoir, mainly because it is that which is interpreting the channeling. This is the part of ourselves that we want to develop and put into action.

The interesting thing is that the more you spend flight time using the IAPSM, the more doorways you can find to it. There is no singular technique. It is good to continually look for different ways to access it. Otherwise it becomes mechanical, uninteresting and eventually inaccessible. If any one method is used too often, something that was at one time a door can become a wall.

STOPPING THOUGHTS, VS., SPACING OUT & DREAMING

There is such a difference between stopping thoughts and creative imagination as opposed to that of spacing out and daydreaming. In the former, you have the self awareness that you are doing so, in the latter, you might as well be dreaming.

As far as dreaming goes, there are a lot of theories about how we can change things in our sleep. But I ask you, if we have a hard enough time changing things when we have full consciousness, how can we change things in our sleep? Even if we could, why waste the time when you could get more done when you are awake? Maybe down the road, you might be able to actualize change in your sleep and work on it later. In the meantime you will get further by picking the readily accessible lower fruit of working on yourself during your waking hours. Later you might get to a point in personal growth where you can undertake the more daunting immediate task of changing something in your sleep.

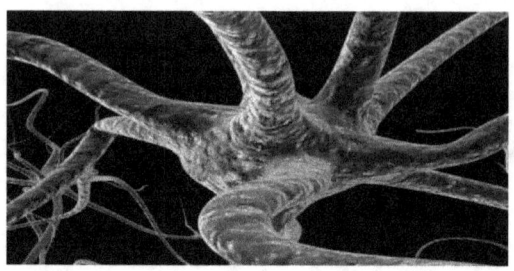

DILATING NEURAL PATHWAYS

The brain functions normally with electrical impulses that travel through nerve pathways in the brain. As we learn something new, there are additional physiological events that are occurring in the brain. An electrical impulse leaps from one part of the neural brain pathways to another part. As we continue to learn something (like memorization, for example), the electrical impulse grows stronger and, with frequency, the pathway gets widened and forms more side pathways like a tree limb. Finally, a new strong neural connection is made. This is called synaptic development.

If we speed things up and take in large amounts of information, there are multiple pathways of electrical impulses leaping and branching out from one part of the brain to another. At certain times the amount of information is so massive and the electricity builds up to such a crescendo that it forces the brain to expand rapidly which transmits so much electricity, it is like getting an electrical shock. At that point we can't think of anything for a few moments (usually accompanied by a reaction of frustration). This is called Brain Fry.

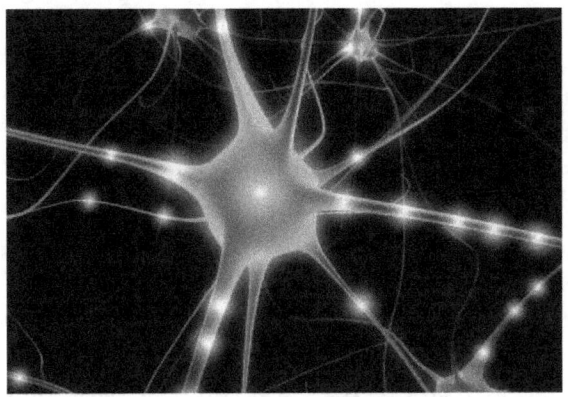

In the process of thinking holographically, we are increasing the level and incidence of Brain Fry. We are making more simultaneous synapse connections. That is because we are thinking three dimensionally and, to do that requires a higher order of thinking (the same way a computer needs more Random Access Memory, RAM, capacity to run concurrent sophisticated programs). The interesting thing about this process is that, when we frequently experience new patterning in our brains, we find that we become somewhat addicted to the experience.

Yes, with these increased number of neural pathways opened, the brain begins to give off endorphins, and then we want to experience more and more of this stimulation. At this point it is hard to turn back, and why should we? It's legal, safe and completely natural!

The experience of increasing intelligence in this manner is so enjoyable that we tend to pursue holographic events insatiably. In all my classes where these methods were taught, either in design classes or improvisational theater, almost all the participants had the same reaction: they wanted more and more. This particular way of thinking can open our eyes to such a degree of illumination that it makes it very difficult to want to shut them again.

Make note, not everyone that has come to my classes has stayed. This is not for everyone. It takes a concerted effort to stay with it the first few times you experience Brain Fry. It's not that it hurts, but it is like the sensation of exercising a particular muscle in the gym. Like anything that is learned, it means pushing ourselves beyond our comfort zones.

Usually when people come in contact with Brain Fry, they give up and stop thinking about the subject that is causing the Brain Fry and thus resort to a substitute for further thinking called "unquestioning belief." Resting, then attempting the specific task over and over will eventually allow you to breakthrough and access what you are trying to access and expand your brain's capacity a little more each time.

FREEDOM OF EXPRESSION

Freedom to express ourselves comes from within, not from without. When it is time to express something, nothing can stop it, except us. It is not necessarily an instantaneous event to be completely free to express yourself simply because you wish to. But sometimes that's all it takes.

When it comes to our internal world, sometimes just wishing to be free is all that is necessary to be free. It is the foundation of creative freedom. Other times we make such a big deal about the process saying, "I have to process this, I have to process that, I'm still in the process of, etc."

My observation is that the need to process is mostly in the mind, not in the necessary action. When there is enough pressure put into a given situation, freedom of expression can become spontaneous. Processing things in our minds over and over tends to become self-indulgent. The more time we have, the more time we have to find obstacles to keep us from doing things.

CREATIVE PRESSURE

With proper training we can learn how to function under creative pressure and thus evoke Holographic Thinking. This is why improvisational techniques are so important. Improvisational techniques can enable us to skip over a lot of potential obstacles, like a hydrofoil skims over the water.

When I was teaching at the Academy of Art University in San Francisco, I had two different conceptual design classes. I gave the same exact design problem to them. The first class was given ten minutes to solve it; the second class, I gave a week. The ones who had ten minutes to solve it did it in ten minutes, no questions asked. The ones, who had a week, came back with all kinds of problems and questions. The next week I reversed the situation between the two classes. The same results happened. You see, with the creative pressure, it got done and even better than when there was little creative pressure.

Why is that?

Because Holographic Thinking is the doorway to the IAPSM that channels and gets to the solution before self judgment gets to obstruct the whole process.

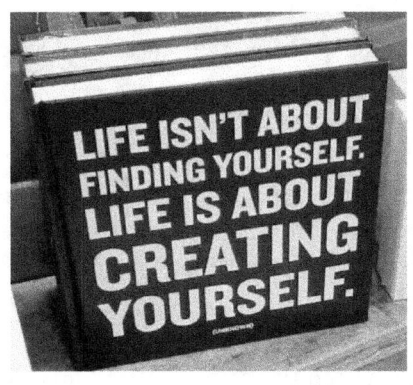

CREATIVE OBSTACLES

There will always be creative obstacles. It goes with the territory. There is no creative or innovative person that didn't have to struggle to get their ideas and inventions out into the world.

The world of "formatory thinking humans" doesn't want change; it doesn't want to have to rethink things. It wants familiarity at all costs.

Some people will stay in very abusive situations, be it a relationship, a partner, a spouse, a neighborhood or a job. They do this even if their very lives are in danger. This is simply because their fear of the unknown and change is a greater pain than the pain they experience every day.

For whatever reason, there is a rite of passage for anyone channeling any new idea. The greater the idea, the greater the challenge is. Look at what Copernicus and Galileo had to endure for their ideas. They never realized the utterly profound contribution they made to our perception of the universe.

Most contributors of great ideas were only discovered long after their death. So the bottom line is whatever you are trying to channel and introduce to the world, you better find the idea greater than whatever kind of reward you expect to gain.

This does not mean we can't get a reward in our lives (i.e., Steve Jobs), but the rewards may not necessarily come with fireworks. Even Jobs had some business challenges and serious painful health problems leading to his premature death.

In my own situation writing this book, I am struggling with some serious, uncomfortable health issues. As an architect, I would consistently have something either physically or circumstantially happen around me before I would start a new project. When I needed to draw something, many times I would get mosquito bites on the end of my fingers. When I was writing about creating things while feeling good and having a positive attitude or teaching a comedy class, there would suddenly be something upsetting that would happen at that time in my life. Sound familiar?

We hear about people all the time that, before they became successful at something, had to live out of their car. Bach had twenty children; now those were some potential distractions. Beethoven went deaf. Leonardo da Vinci had to eke out a living and, even when he had a commission to invent or paint something, he would find a way to secretly study or create something else he was actually interested in and felt compelled to do. Socrates and Buddha were poisoned; Einstein had to flee Germany and sacrifice his Noble Peace Prize money to get free to do what he felt he needed to do.

Having an excuse for not doing something you feel compelled to do because of some obstacle in your way is not a real excuse. You can always take some comfort in knowing that in taking a creative risk, you are in good company.

Now this doesn't mean that, in order to learn how to think on a higher level, you must sacrifice your right arm or firstborn. It just means that the little discomfort you might experience, from yourself and others, to think your own thoughts and to do what you are compelled to do, is nothing compared to those who have gone before you. Not only that, I have made the process of contacting and functioning from your higher mind very simple.

Remember this: effort begins with an "Eh!"

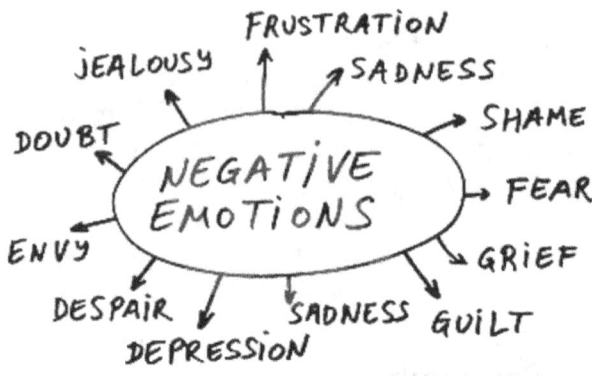

NEGATIVE EMOTIONS

There is probably no more of a creative wet blanket and obstacle to higher thinking than negative emotions. It clouds your thinking and is the biggest indicator of subjectivity. The best thing to do is to transform those negative emotions, and there are a lot of misnomers about how this is accomplished. Negative emotions are also an indicator of something you need to look at in yourself to see why you are feeling negative.

The most important thing to remember is that no one or nothing makes us negative; we are responsible for our own negative emotions and their transformation, and the most difficult negative emotions to get rid of are the ones we are the most justified in having.

The main source of negative emotions is usually our imaginary picture, and expectations of what should happen and then doesn't. It is also often the result of a situation that reveals our hypocrisy and contradictions. This, by the way, is where the Brain Games are invaluable.

What are negative emotions?

Here are some examples:

Fear, anger, disgust, envy, indifference, inferiority, sadness, complaining, anxiousness, feeling duped, disappointment, grief, humiliation, intimidation, worry and feeling sorry for yourself.

Everyone experiences negative emotions to some degree or another. If you find someone who says they do not, they are lying. That does not mean that there are not people who are proficient at transforming their negative emotions better than others; but it does mean that we all have them, and they can actually propel us to transforming our consciousness and awareness.

There are as many ways to transform negative emotions as there are negative emotions. The most important thing about transforming them is to first recognize you are experiencing them and then be willing to transform them.

One thing for sure that is not only worthless but is actually dangerous to your health, is to ignore them entirely and put on a false happy face and pretend you are just fine. That is not transformation but suppression. Sometimes letting off some immediate steam, like saying "ouch" when you get hurt, can be useful, as long as it does not turn into a temper tantrum.

Suffering is the source of negative emotions. There is necessary suffering and unnecessary suffering. If a brick falls on your foot and it hurts, that is necessary suffering. If you complain and whine about it over and over again, that is unnecessary suffering.

What are some ways to transform negative emotions?

Everything I describe about how to cleanse your magnetic field is mostly about transforming negative emotions that have created an abstracted magnetic field in us. However, there are some additional ways, and one that stands out is talking out what is making you feel negative, with someone willing to listen, and then be done with it.

The difference between talking about what is making you negative (to cleanse your mind and emotions) and complaining, is how many times and how long you keep doing it. If you have to tell any one person more than once or to tell more than three people, it has become complaining. This may not do the trick, but there is one other thing that works, whether you can tell others or not.

Every time you start to discuss whatever subject that has you tweaked, take a deep breath, while feeling and experiencing what is tweaking you deeply, then blow out your breath and let whatever is bothering or hurting you disperse into the air. Do this a few times if you have to, but don't expect it to completely go away. Some things are so big we can't eliminate them all at once, but one breath at a time. So let go of it as much as you can with the exhaled breath and deal with it again later. Benjamin Franklin said, "Little strokes fell great oaks."

Basically, negative emotions are the result of a lack of understanding about something. As long as you feel negative, you will have little ability to think objectively. The irony is, the way out of feeling negative is to think more objectively.

In order to do this, we need to go back to the expression: "Are you your eyes or that which is looking out of your eyes?" Are you your emotions and thoughts or that which is observing your emotions and thoughts?

In order to transform, you must think objectively and, as you read all the rest of what I am writing about, you need to remember that who you are is not of the body, mind or feelings, but something that observes and is separate from those things. This is the one of the best ways getting you out of your funk.

If you are feeling stressed about something, then you have not transformed you negative emotions about it. Time to cleanse you magnetic field.

Here is a good example:

I was once in line at a restaurant, waiting to order something, when I felt someone kick me from behind. I was immediately angry and wanted to turn around to do, I don't know what. When I did turn around, I looked down to see a three-year-old wearing the same kind of camouflage pants I was wearing. He smiled at me, and I could immediately see it was his way to let me know that he was a big boy, wearing the same pants, and he wanted to get my attention and let me know that. My anger immediately turned into humor and good feelings.

This is a great example of how negative emotions are an illusion and a lack of understanding of some bigger idea of which we are not aware. It is a great example of having something in me that could, at that moment, observe and see things more objectively.

ACCEPTING CRITICISM

You already know that you are your own worst critic. It is in all of us, and it is what prevents us from accessing our full potential.

"Access to our higher minds is already available to us. We just have to learn how to stop censoring ourselves."

A good creative attitude involves positive receptivity of new ideas. It eliminates self-judgment and enables one to visualize and to use criticism as a tool for looking at what one is doing from a different perspective.

Criticism from others really forces us to look at ourselves. Let's face it, most creative things that we do are for our own personal fulfillment. When we are creating something, it is an expression of a part of us. Even if we create something for someone else, we still need a sense of self-satisfaction.

Without that sense of self-satisfaction, many partnerships and marriages have broken up.

Really, each time we create something we do it in order for us to see and examine something about ourselves. This is an inherent benefit to being creative. It is very difficult to find an artist that doesn't have some self-examining philosophical inclination. If you aren't sure if they are looking at themselves, criticize them a little and see what happens.

When you create from inspiration, that experience does not care about criticism, from within or without. The artist is channeling and knows it is not him or her that is coming up with the idea. Should someone make a comment about what they are doing, they can step back, look at themselves and re-evaluate whatever they are doing. Sometimes it merits a change and sometimes not.

SELF JUDGMENT

Creativity exists in us naturally. Observe any child. If you ask them to make up a story or draw a picture or sing a song or make up a dance, they just do it with little or no hesitation. As adults, problems arise, as things in our own personalities have formed over time that obstructs our ability and willingness to do these things. Some picture of us has formed that says, "You can't do this or that." All these small pictures added up and result in an imaginary Self-Picture. This imaginary Self-Picture creates a defensive personality and is the source of self-judgment.

Often, I hear the comment, "I find it hard to look at myself because I'm afraid of what I might see!" My response to this is, "What the heck do you expect to see? There's nothing there!" In other words there is no monster lurking in the dark, except the monster that wants to judge what it sees.

Be aware that self pity is a way to justify not changing yourself.

Here is a rule of thumb about self-observation:

The level of fear of seeing ourselves diminishes in proportion to the amount of real time that we actually see ourselves. To put it another way, some people say they are looking at themselves and are stressed about it. However, I can guarantee you that the stress is due to a prolonged fear of avoiding looking at themselves, rather than the actual doing of it.

Be forgiving of yourself. If you see something you don't like or feel good about, clarify your basic intentions, make the necessary adjustments and continue on your journey. Lamenting and self-judging is procrastination instead of action. Having a forgiving attitude toward oneself is a dimension of self confidence. This doesn't mean that all the criticism we get is going to be easy to take, but it does mean that we can recover faster from it and transform difficult criticism into useful information.

APPROVAL FROM OTHERS

This self-judgment is perpetuated because of the need to be liked and accepted. We tend to listen to everyone even if we try not to. How many times has someone said things to us and we responded by walking away and shutting them off, only to find their words still rattling around in our head hours or days later?

Isn't rebellion the opposite half of the same idea as conformity? On many occasions in rebelling against my parents I would say to myself, "If my father really knew why I was doing this, he would approve." There I was, still seeking approval; even though I thought I was being my own person.

Doing things free from the need of others' approval is a skillful endeavor. Being able to do things free of parental approval is the rite of passage from childhood to adulthood. A clear and self-forgiving attitude about ourselves helps us to become courageous about putting ourselves into the spotlight. A more whimsical attitude helps us not take ourselves so seriously.

ELIMINATING SELF JUDGMENT

When it comes to expressing ourselves, no idea is taboo! As individuals, our creative imagination is a thread woven into some much larger tapestry. We just don't know where it will lead us. That is precisely what makes creativity so exciting. If we start to do something, we need to feel free to express whatever pops into our heads. Maybe it's that "silly something" that doesn't seem to relate at all to what we're supposed do. Maybe it's the artistic expression of that certain fantasy. It doesn't matter; it's just leading us to where we need to go. To suppress or judge it, prevents us from discovering something significant in ourselves and progressing to a new level of consciousness.

No matter what pops into our heads, it's good to record it and observe it, but not to judge it. We analyze things too early and with limited observations.

An observation is like a drop of water. You can tell a lot from a drop of water: it's H_2O, colorless, tasteless, conducts electricity with impurities in it, etc.

However with only one drop of water we could never know about waves.

It is the waves that really affect us and show us our patterns and many drops of water reveal these patterns. So it is with observation. If we observe our expressions without judging or forming a conclusion about them, we will be able to see patterns and these patterns are also always changing.

Really it is almost a complete waste of time to analyze or judge what comes out of us. Just keep on going! Most of the time we are just clearing out thoughts rattling around in our heads and there is relatively no significance to them. The best thing to do is to just express them, and they're gone.

> There is the story of the two monks who had vowed not to have any kind of contact with women in order to keep focused on their spiritual path. One day, as they were about to cross a stream, they saw a woman fearful to cross it herself. She asked if one of the monks would help her across. The first monk picked her up and carried her to the other side.

A few miles later the second monk said to the first monk, "How could you violate our vow to not touch women and carry that woman across the stream?" The first monk replied, "I left that woman at the other side of the stream. You are still carrying her."

When it comes to creative expression, whatever pops out are just things that pop out. Don't worry about what other people may think and make a big psychoanalysis out of it. Just keep on expressing until you get to what you are looking for. Every creative endeavor needs to have a warm-up; just let the ideas start flowing, before you know it you will become a visionary.

HOW QUICKLY DO YOU GET UP AGAIN?

Johann Goethe said:

"It doesn't matter how many time you fall, but how quickly you can get back up again that counts."

Or, get back on the horse and keep going.

A good example of this is:

I once saw a young cellist performing in concert. He was actually the student of a very great cellist. When he played, he had so much love for the sound of that cello. Every sound was as if he were hugging and squeezing sweet nectar out of the cello. As I sat and listened, a most interesting thing happened. He made a mistake; the bow made a kind of scratchy, wimpy start at the note.

Instead of covering up or quickly glossing over the mistake, he loved the mistake. He caressed the mistake and extended the scratchy, wimpy sound, and led it into a beautiful, sustained note. It was so beautiful that I hoped he would make another mistake and another one.

It was as if each mistake was actually the cello crying about some great, deep suffering it had to endure. You could tell he loved that instrument and every sound it made, even the scratchy ones. That was why he was able to play so beautifully. He could see clearly that the scratchy mistake was part of the foundation of producing a beautiful sound.

He had a positive immediate reaction to the unexpected in his instrument and he knew he didn't have to be perfect, He was able to thrive on the unexpected and turn it into something unique and beautiful.

WHAT IS SELF CONFIDENCE?

Self confidence is not about being right all the time. It is not about acting as if you have your act together either, because that is an act. Self confidence is about knowing that you can be wrong or make a mistake, laugh at yourself about it and move on.

Even the best and most successful performers have moments of stage fright and the fear of making mistakes. The main difference between them and an inexperienced performer is that the professional has had more flight time in getting past that stage fright and improvising when a mistake is made. They have positive, successful images of themselves overcoming obstacles that they will inevitably encounter as part of their performance.

Therefore, they just perform anyway, knowing that the stage fright will dissipate when they start and that they will just deal with the unexpected as it happens. This is true for any situation in which we feel we are expected to be successful.

There is, however, a method that can minimize or even eliminate the fear of mistakes and self-judgment. This method involves the substitution of bad feelings associated with failure with the feelings of good humor, and the exhilaration of new beginnings and fresh starts. This technique redirects our honest reactions to mistakes into competent actions.

HERE ARE TEN BASIC RULES OF CREATIVITY AND SELF CONFIDENCE:

I. DARE TO FAIL

II. DARE TO START OVER

III. DARE TO ALWAYS BE A BEGINNER

IV. DARE TO BE SIMPLE

V. DARE TO BE SHY AND AWKWARD

VI. DARE TO START WITHOUT A PLAN

VII. DARE TO BE COMPLETELY IDIOTIC AND FOOLISH

VIII. DARE TO CHANGE YOUR MIND

IX. DARE NOT TO SUCCEED

X. DARE TO END

I. Dare To Fail.

Dare to fail as often as possible. Start to re-associate the word and experience of *failure* with an experience of exhilaration. Begin to see failure as nothing more than a transition from an expected reality to an unexpected one, as a doorway rather than a wall. The worst you can do is stumble. Real failure is taking too much time to pick yourself up.

Should you find yourself taking too much time, just get up and:

II. Dare to Start Over.

Start over without any of the baggage of any previous experience. Get right back up on that horse and ride.

See yourself fresh, innocent and-.

III. Dare to Always Be a Beginner

I don't care how long you have done something; you can always experience being a beginner. You can always empty yourself. In Zen Buddhism it's called "emptying your cup." Creativity comes through you, not from you. No matter how long it has been coming through you, and, since it is not you, it can always be seen as a miraculous new experience. It is just like seeing a newborn baby coming from "who knows where" with an entire life and fate of its own.

The way to be a beginner is to:

IV. Dare To Be Simple.

Don't be clever. Don't try to "do." Be simple and basic; let your mind wander. Don't indulge the feeling of the need to control or to perform. Things get complex all on their own.

Be innocent and, if you feel unsure, then:

V. Dare to Be Shy and Awkward.

The best remedy for being unsure, shy or awkward is to perform that way without judging yourself. You will see that, when you express these feelings, you can empower yourself very easily. If your task is to publicly speak, by admitting to the audience that you are nervous, you can evoke empathy. This can create a certain kind of bonding that should be the main objective of a public speaker in order to get their point of view across. Some of the best public speakers, intentionally, don't think specifically about what they are going to say in order to create that spontaneous empathetic audience response.

This brings us to the next idea-

VI. Dare to Start Without a Plan.

Get into trouble right away! Before mountain climbers climb a mountain, they might study the mountain to figure out the best way up. When they are actually climbing the mountain, small crevices that seemed unimportant at the bottom of the rock face become very important, and the mountain climber becomes very creative with these crevices, as they make their way up to the top using them.

Sometimes, intentionally, putting oneself in a restricted situation may be just what is necessary to evoke a certain texture or uniqueness to approaching a situation creatively. When trying to come up with something fresh and new, don't think. "JUST DO IT!" Start.

You don't have to be good to start; you just have to start to be good.

Everything is connected in some way or another. Simply wishing to go in a particular direction is all one really needs to get started.

In fact-

VII. Dare to Be Completely Idiotic and Foolish

I'm sure that everyone has had the experience of trying to figure something out, struggling and struggling. Finally it hits you: it was so simple! And you say to yourself, "What an idiot I've been!" It is precisely at this moment that we have the opportunity to experience great intelligence. It is then that possibilities open up for us. This is because real knowing starts out with the realization that we don't know. Become an empty vessel so that new things can fill us.

Do the first thing that comes to mind no matter how silly it may seem. You would be amazed at what ingenious, wonderful things have grown out of seemingly, the most ridiculous ideas. Don't be afraid of being called weird or crazy. It's the really crazy people that are afraid to admit it. Everyone is a little quirky and should feel free to admit it. It is the really sick people that are always trying to appear "normal."

As the Mad Hatter, in *Alice in Wonderland* said:

"We are all mad here."

Have the courage to:

VIII. Dare to Change Your Mind.

Dare to Change Your Mind and, as Walt Whitman said, "I contradict myself." I like to think of it with a parody of that public emergency statement that we hear on the radio in mind, "Life is a test. It is only a test. Had this been a real life, we would know where to go and what to do." Don't set yourself up to be infallible. When you create that kind of scenario for yourself, you start to isolate from more and more people in order to keep up some perfect self-image. This is an accident waiting to happen; if left to continue too long, it leads to extreme thinking and major psychological problems.

It is actually better to:

IX. Dare Not to Succeed.

Don't try so hard that you lose your sense of whimsy and flexibility. When it comes to new ideas, it is important not to take either the idea or yourself too seriously. By maintaining a whimsical attitude, you can be open to more ideas and suggestions. You won't get lost and bogged down in your own self-indulgence. There are many versions of any idea. Why limit yourself? Limiting youself is largely what leads to creative blocks. Ideas have a certain life of their own. Learn how to be sensitive to this. "Don't work hard, work easy." You can run much farther relaxed than tense.

This does not mean you can't **Dare to Succeed** too. No, it just means don't get so immersed in the idea of succeeding, that you miss the point of what you are doing to begin with.

"Life is about the journey, not the destination" Why? It is because every destination is the beginning of a new journey. If you just live for the destination you will never reach it and life will pass you by.

Finally:

X. Dare To End.

Recognize that each idea has its time when it is relevant and its time when it has played out its course. Many creative things in life are like music where there is a movement and a rest. Things can be short, sweet and relevant and that's it!

NEXT

INSPIRATION

All of the things I have been talking about so far can be understood for the most part, through having the experience of inspiration. This psychological state of inspiration includes Holographic Thinking, out-of-the-box thinking, channeling and so many other elements. The only thing that is added to this experience is that of also being an "observer," stepping back and, from this state of inspiration, seeing it as a process that we are simply witnessing.

Even though Holographic Thinking can be experienced through inspiration, the ability of being the observer is actually something much more. Basically it entails the ideas that I am sharing, with an additional higher emotional element involved, called Conscious Inspiration.

The whole point of what I am talking about is to facilitate methods that show your how to achieve the state of inspiration more often, have longer endurance of it and to take you far deeper into the experience of it that would normally happen.

Here you are being shown here all the elements that go into inspiration and, through the brain games and exercises, the elusive final ingredient of inspiration will tend to arrive more frequently. In other words, it is the reverse engineering of inspiration while functioning and producing things at the highest level.

Inspiration produces a different chemistry in us, and the converse is true: if you reproduce the chemistry, you have a chance at producing inspiration.

You will learn what produces the reverse engineering of the chemistry of inspiration by doing the exercises that you will be shown later in this book.

HIGHER EMOTIONS

Some people refer to higher emotions as emotional intelligence. So what does that mean?

There are three basic groups of emotions:

The first category is **instinctive emotions** which are based on sentimentality, crowd emotions, emotions that honor national pride; the appreciation of cute animals; finding holidays and family to be very important.

The second category is **extreme emotions**. These are emotions that feel intense love in relationships, but these emotions can also be overly sensitive and volatile: I love you one moment; I hate you the next, then back to love again. These emotions also have the ability to be very perceptive about people. However, many times they jump to conclusions too soon on "snapshots of just one moment" in a person's life, and not the whole person's being and intent. When experiencing extreme emotions, individuals need to remember that waves are what count and not the many drops of water.

The third category is **creative emotions,** which are related to art and all of its aspects. They are about aestheticism and sacrificing one's personal comfort for some idea or creation that is bigger than oneself.

These creative emotions are the higher emotional elements which inspire us to be inspired in the first place. This is a very rare experience or nonexistent for many people. Yet it is those individuals that function with this kind of emotion that we celebrate or call our heroes. The Founding Fathers of the United States were motivated from their higher emotions.

Just think what an amazing world we would live in if more people would lead their lives from this noble place. Although we all have the other emotions in us, and they have their respective value, these higher inspired emotions as the primary focus can change your life as well as others for the better.

STARTING-UP CREATIVITY

There are different methods of creating. No one method is an absolute. Here are some proven ways of starting the creative process that have worked for me and my students.

Getting started can sometimes be the hardest thing to do. We will do almost anything rather than begin. One of the main things that keep us from getting started is fear of failure. Rather than experiencing failure, we will start failing before we get a chance to actually do so. We sabotage before we even start by engaging in self-criticism. If you find you are criticizing yourself, you are most likely procrastinating. Just begin!

Life is hard. There are things that happen to us that rattle around in our minds and interfere with our creativity. It is important to establish your very own creative haven where no one and nothing can disturb you. It is important to actually create some kind of ritual (no matter how seemingly insignificant) that enables you to dump the internal dialogue and trash. This is also vitally important when creating with others. If you have a disagreement with someone you are creating with, discuss it, argue it or duke it out (just kidding) before entering your creative haven.

When you enter your creative haven, create a ritual that will leave your troubles at the door.

Serious vs. Whimsical

There are more creative possibilities with a whimsical, creative attitude than with a serious one. It's not that it's impossible to accomplish the same ends with a serious attitude, but, because we are only human, when we take on a serious attitude, we are less likely to accept criticism from others and tend to fear failure more. This closes us off to possibilities rather than opening us to them.

When we have a whimsical attitude, we can see more possibilities and can take in more ideas. Then we have more to choose from later when we come back and see all the ideas we have generated. When a person creates seriously, they tend to get stuck on one idea. Besides, it is less fun.

Finding Time to Be Creative and Actually Think about Things:

If you feel you don't have time to work on your creative projects, you're not alone; you're in some great company. People like Leonardo da Vinci, Mozart, Bach (who had the distraction of his twenty children) and scores of other inventors and entrepreneurs had to carve out time in their lives to work on their own creative projects.

Sometimes it meant losing sleep, money, spouses or friends. Somehow they managed to do it because they were driven to make the time. Sometimes you just have to take the gamble. At least this kind of gamble is based on something you believe in: yourself.

Creativity Is a State of Mind:

What we specifically do creatively is irrelevant, as long as we can understand that creativity is a state of mind. If we can get into this inspired state of mind we can apply it to any situation, even mowing the lawn. What we end up creating is insignificant compared to achieving that inspirational state of mind. What we create is the byproduct of this higher state of mind. The actual product itself was really a diversion from the high creative state of mind. But that's OK. That is how things work.

Wishing to Be Creative Is a Creative Act:

This is always the beginning of creativity. If we wish it enough, we will get there. Again, like Benjamin Franklin said; "Little strokes fell great oaks." Each small effort to get back on a creative track adds up eventually, so it is important to not put yourself under pressure. A snake cannot just rip off its own skin just any old time. It needs to wait until it is time for it to shed. With constant effort, desire and patience, things will eventually click, and you will be inspired again.

In the meantime, play different creative games; find a new tool to work with.

For example:

In music, with the invention of synthesizers, experimenting with new sounds or drum beats can inspire a new kind of music.

In art, maybe a new pencil, pen, brush, canvas etc. can bring about something fresh and new.

In design, a new computer program can change everything.

In writing, use your own handwriting if you always use a computer or vice versa; record your voice or use voice recognition software; record your conversation with another person; draw or doodle a picture of what you are trying to communicate, etc.

In short, get out of your usual way of doing things.

Don't Compare Your Creativity with Someone Else's:

You have your own creative life style and it is, in the long run, the experience of creativity, not the product that counts. It is not what talent you don't have that matters; it's what you do with the talent you do with it that counts.

If you have a thimbleful of fuel and yet can travel a thousand miles, and someone has a gas tanker of fuel and travels the same distance, what is the greater experience? If your simple, efficient use of fuel got you the experience you need, why lust after the tanker of fuel?

If the tanker of fuel represents the need to be popular and famous, then you are operating from the wrong place. Besides, most significant people in history were not recognized in their own time. The converse is also true; some people that were recognized in their own time are insignificant now.

It is important to be of assistance to the world and not expect the world to be of assistance to you. You can have goals, but they are simply a direction to travel, while the real destination reveals itself during your journey. You must learn to enjoy and to find a way to make your journey into an adventure and to not be fixated on your goal. The real goal of our life's adventure is most likely not what we usually expect. Show me one person now, or throughout history, who knew for sure where they would end up.

Restricting or Limiting Creativity Can Bring out More of It:

There is something in us that is completely willful. If we are not allowed to do something, we automatically want to do it. In learning tennis, one technique that teaches how to place a ball on a spot on the other side of the net is to try "not to hit the spot." Try to be completely frivolous creatively and you might find yourself getting intense. Try to be serious, and you might find yourself doing something very goofy.

Believe it or not, crime can be a creative act. Haven't you seen a crime that was committed and said, "How in the world did they think of that?" Yes, crime can be a creative outlet from a desperate lack of creative and productive opportunity. It shows how creativity can thrive, even in the face of adversity and restriction.

If you want to get out of your creative funk, sometimes by using three colors instead of eight, which can create intentional restrictions, may be a vehicle to break free of a blockage.

Diversify Creative Projects:

"Don't put all your creative eggs in one basket." Do a number of different creative things at the same time. Take breaks from one and work on another one. For example, I stop painting or drawing to play music to relieve any unnecessary pressure I have put on myself.

Diversifying your creative endeavors opens up the possibilities of finding new design tools for other creative projects. It can be a new way to look at things.

For example:

I found a new way to view and design architecture when I read Johann Goethe's quote that, "Architecture is like frozen music." Another one is the architect Louis Kahn who asked, "What do you want brick?" And brick responds, "I'd like an arch."

Leonardo da Vinci would work on several projects at a time. This way he would always be productive; when a circumstance would prohibit him from continuing on one project, he would work on a second or third project. Then when circumstances changed, he would go back to work on the first project and so on.

Taking Breaks:

When they were first starting out to paint or draw, I would to tell my students to only work for twenty minutes at a time; to set an alarm clock if they needed to and to keep this as a discipline. This enables them to see their project with a fresh perspective. I even told them to work on their drawing upside down sometimes.

The same thing is true with thinking and giving birth to new ideas. People tend to give up on thinking about things too easily. People get to the point of "Brain Fry" and give up, when all they need to do is rest, try again, rest, try again, until eventually, there will be a breakthrough. This is how Einstein worked on his ideas. He would visualize, rest and visualize again, until he had a breakthrough.

ELIMINATING CREATIVE BLOCKS

The main reason people experience creative blocks is because they learn to be creative or think in only one or two ways. Every creative way has its own life span, and, when it runs out, it runs out. If you are not prepared with another way to be creative, you are stumped. It is important to learn how to be creative in many ways and to know how to invent new ways of being creative.

I have over 1,200 creative games. Each one of them yields its own results. Each one of them speaks to people in different ways, some more effectively than others. But, beyond a doubt, there is something for everyone.

Even the most talented people will eventually have creative blocks, because their game's life span ran out. We see this in every creative endeavor from writing, music, painting, to fashion design, architecture and invention. People identify themselves with their form of creation and, because of that, can't step away from themselves and their egos to look at themselves and what they are doing differently.

It is easier to train someone from scratch on how to constantly reinvent themselves and never run out of ideas than someone who has been very successful at something and has run into a creative block, but it is still possible.

This is true mainly because, since ideas don't come from us but through us and the cosmos of ideas is infinite, a person with a creative block just needs to renew themselves, become a new soft piece of clay and start over.

PROGRAMMING YOURSELF

At the beginning of a project, start by taking in all the information, both the general and significant details. Then get a good night's sleep, and start the project in the morning. Your Inner Mind is already working on the solution while you sleep or while you are preoccupied with other things.

There are automatic functions in our brains that work all on their own, calculating, analyzing, planning and doing it without our commentary and self-judgment. As you study this over time, you will eventually find that there is very little that goes on in us that can't function that way on its own without our constant voices in our heads dominating the experience. In fact, you can eventually see that the only thing we need to do is observe all that is going on.

IMITATION AND ACCIDENT

Imitating someone or something you admire is sometimes a good place to start. It's like learning how to dance. First you learn the steps, and then you mix and recombine them. The next thing you know, you're accidentally combining them in new ways, and there you are, inventing a new dance step.

The important part, though, is to remember that imitation is only a starting place. Great thoughts and creations of all incarnations mostly come into existence not because they were planned, they came into being because who ever had discovered these ideas and inventions was able to have the consciousness to recognize the results of something that occurred accidentally.

So the next time you think something is a mistake, it is more likely a door of opportunity.

BRAIN GAMES"

OBJECTIVE THINKING EXERCISES

In order to think "out of the box" and think objectively, we need to become aware of our habitual mechanical behavior.

How is this done?

1. By first being able to see what it is that is mechanical, then finding a way to change it. There are several ways of doing this. The most effective way is by doing improvisation brain games with others. But this can also be done by yourself by consistently changing your routines, daily, weekly, monthly, etc.

a) Go to a new place for coffee in the morning.

b) Drink tea instead of coffee one morning or two a week.

c) Walk somewhere instead of driving.

d) Doing something different with your hair.

e) Make a new friend out of your typical social tribe.

f) Use your other hand to eat.

g) Put your keys or money in a different pocket.

Make up your own change of habit, experiments.

2. Another way to develop new thoughts is to learn how to accept difficult challenges, "making a silk purse out of a sow's ear." In my improvisational theater classes, I use an exercise where I have the first performer offer the second performer the most awful thing they can possibly imagine. The second performer then says, "Thank you" (as if it was the best idea they ever got in their entire life) and instantly finds some positive way to use this offer. If you can learn how to do this, you will be amazed at how much your brain activity will increase. For example:

a) OFFER - Here is some lint from my bellybutton.

RESPONSE - Thank you. I need more lint for my yarn ball.

b) OFFER - Here is some horse manure.

RESPONSE - Thank you. I need that for my collection at the science show. (I didn't say that the responses had to be good, just transforming)

c) OFFER- Here is some earwax.

RESPONSE - Thank you. I was running out of surfboard wax.

d) OFFER - Here is a rusty battery I found.

RESPONSE - Thank you. Now I can contribute something to the recycle center.

It can be endless.

3. A third exercise is to take two or more things that don't go together and make them somehow work together; the more difficult, the better. Ask someone else to come up with the choices to make sure you are not going easy on yourself. You can also create, with friends or by yourself, a whole collection of different words, write them on individual slips of paper and draw them from a hat.

Here are some games:

a) Make up an ad or commercial that has what you want to sell, but add something that has nothing to do with what you want to sell. This is something advertisers use a lot these days and was derived from improvisational theater games.

For example:

You want to sell golf balls and you have to fit in high heeled shoes into your pitch:

"Ladies and Gentleman, I have found that trying to hit a great golf shot without our specially designed golf balls is harder than teeing off in high heel shoes."

b) Use three hats or containers:

First hat - Different locations in the world

Second hat - Styles of architecture or design

Third hat - A type of building, like a school, store, house, office, car wash, bus stop, any physical place.

Now make up a way to use all three items. For example:

I will use: Car wash +Tuscan + San Francisco

I draw or describe a vision of a car wash with Tuscan columns and the car wash attendants wearing togas and wearing big glasses like computer geeks.

c) Make up a limerick with two completely random words drawn from a hat. For example:

The words "track" and "Spam."

I once found myself on a **"track"**

I must have just fallen on my back.

I opened some **"Spam"**

And away I ran

And now I must sleep on a sack.

Just do something different. You will learn three things:

1. You will find out how comfort and familiarity controls your thinking and how hard it is to change one small routine. This is what perpetuates formatory thinking and is the biggest barrier to higher thinking.

2. If you are successful at breaking your routines, you will see how much more conscious you are becoming and see how other people are stuck in their routines. You will see how most people operate mechanically and why few people use their brains for actually thinking instead of just giving a preprogrammed stimulus-response reaction.

3. You will see how you start thinking differently than others and your behavior will change for the better.

TEAMWORK GAME GUIDELINES

Virtually nothing can be more accelerating in inducing Holographic Thinking, Brain Fry, and mind expansion than doing group exercises. This is because you really will have to face the live action, in the moment, with unexpected ideas from others as well as yourself. It also will create a good-natured peer pressure, enabling you to go beyond what you would do normally.

When working as a team, work as if you are all neighbors building a barn together. Establish who the barn is for, who is doing what and learn how to support each team member's ideas. Do what needs to be done without concerning yourself about what efforts anyone else is making or their roles. Most of all, make the other team members look good, instead of focusing on yourself.

When working with others think of it like a dance where each dancer tries to be aware of the movements of the other and adjusts accordingly. Think about all the instantaneous adjustments that have to be made. It is amazing that there aren't more accidents, on the dance floor, yet we manage to not make them. If there is some kind of accidental move, we immediately turn it into a new dance step.

The same thing is possible when working with others in a team. If participants are willing, the most complex changes can be dealt with as a team. In the business corporate world, these techniques can create a whole new dynamic.

For example, instead of rewarding the person who makes the most basket shots, you reward the people who make the most assists. This dynamic will get people to work harder to help, rather than to get the most attention. It instantly removes the conflicting egos in the workplace.

Making Offers:

Making an offer simply means offering an idea. It is vital to set up an environment where ideas are encouraged. This doesn't mean that ideas are thrown out willy-nilly all the time. There needs to be a time and place for ideas, and a time to just get down to business.

Accepting Offers:

Have patience. After a team member makes an offer, whether you think it will work or not, see how it could work and include it in the idea as a whole. If you feel that the idea is going in the wrong direction, remember not to use the word "but". Instead, say, "YES, AND IN ADDITION TO THAT."

Make it so that you are adding to an offer, rather than negating it. This is called "endowment and enhancement."

Whimsical Group Mind:

When with a group, maintain a whimsical attitude and leave your personal ego at the door. Remember, when things are serious, we are usually working too hard to control and the ego gets involved, which will evoke other team members' egos.

You can accomplish more and develop additional ideas when you are unattached to them. A whimsical group mind is a good application for Holographic Thinking. This is because when we are thinking holographically, we are seeing ideas spherically instead of linearly. If we see ideas spherically, we are outside of the ideas and can rearrange and compare them.

Arbitrary Plan:

Don't make a big deal out of starting. All plans don't have to have great, deep thoughts in order to become that way. You would be amazed how creative endeavors can get complex all on their own just because there is more than one person involved with them. DARE TO BE SIMPLE. Start anywhere and it will lead you where you want to go, simply because you wish to go there.

Leading a Team:

As a team leader it is important to escort, but not to drive. Stay neutral and set directions. You can do this by setting up restrictions and changing the restrictions when necessary. Don't over-control; just watch what happens, keep the team on track and steer towards the defined goal. Create time limits for an idea to be discussed, but don't be formatory about it and have some flexibility.

The team leader should be the most willing to take on whatever role is necessary to accomplish what needs to be done. Being a team leader is not about more power but about more service to the team. If the floor needs to be swept, you sweep the floors. As the team leader you are the one to bridge the gaps and do what needs to be done that other's miss.

The team leader is the chief barn builder, in charge of keeping the humor and the spirits positive throughout the entire process. From time to time, there are standoffs in a team. This is why it is valuable for the team leader to maintain a neutral posture throughout the whole process. Where there is polarization, the team leader needs to inspire more possibilities rather than taking sides.

The team leader needs to be the one to make the final decision when the team has reached its goal or needs to be pushed further, could use a break, and needs to start over or to simply stop. This is also where staying neutral is important.

TEAM BRAIN GAMES

The following are basic brain games that will guarantee you will expand your brain for a long time. I say a long time because, no matter how complex things are, if we repeat them enough we can adapt and make them mechanical, so new games are necessary.

There are over 1,200 games that I have on file and I seem to find or make up more all the time. However, I doubt if a person could get to them all.

Why? Because you would find that, while on your journey to doing them all, you would most likely get sidetracked and start making up your own, and that's a good thing.

If you still want all 1,200 games, you can contact me through my website: www.mindmavericks.org, and I will send them to you for a small handling fee.

OK, now it is important to do these following games in the sequence that I list them. They are deliberately set up to allow your brain to adjust and not cause you or others to give up and reject the whole thing. Remember, the secret to this method of accessing your Higher Mind is to be able to spend enough flight time in the higher state of mind long enough so that our survival mind learns that the new chemistry is a good thing and is not threatening our survival.

1. STRETCHING - WARMING UP:

Start out by stretching and taking a few deep breaths. Relax and prepare yourself to laugh and have fun. Make funny stupid ridiculous faces and stretch out the game face you wear all the time for others and even yourself.

2. SOUND BALL: A team stands around in a circle. The first person makes a sound and a gesture and throws the ball (making eye contact) to a second person at random, who then imitates the sound and gesture of the first person (while still maintaining eye contact with the first person). Next, the second person turns to a third person at random, makes up their own sound and gesture, throws the ball to the third person (making eye contact) and so on to the fourth, fifth, etc., for about five minutes.

This exercise is designed to warm you up and get you used to expressing yourself freely, without self-judgment.

3. LIGHT-SPEED SOUND BALL: This is the same as regular sound ball, except do it immediately without the very slightest hesitation and I mean react as fast as a half a second at the most. Don't think; just react immediately.

This will definitely blow out the cobwebs in your mind. You will be experiencing the first stage of Holographic Thinking.

4. MULTIPLE SOUND BALLS: This is the same as the light speed sound ball; except someone starts two or three sound balls and you must use your peripheral vision to see all the sound balls at the same time. Be aware that you might be giving and getting a sound ball at the same time.

This, as in all exercises, entails two of the ten basics shared earlier "Dare to Fail, Dare to start over." If you weren't experiencing Holographic Thinking yet, you will surely be doing it now.

5. ONE-WORD STORY: This exercise is done in a circle again and each person takes a turn in whatever order you're standing. Each person can only say one word with the intent of the whole team trying to create a story. Keep going until the story seems to find its own ending. Don't be clever; Dare to Be Simple and just put whatever word into the story that is appropriate in a grammatically correct sentence. This means that the only word any one person might get to say is an "and" or a "the." Try to keep the story simple without putting many twists and turns in it. Having several different people contributing will make it complicated enough.

This exercise is designed to start people listening and working together as a team. It is about co-channeling and staying open and adjusting to the unexpected. Instead of being clever and drawing attention to yourself, make the other team members look good.

6. MULTIPLE-WORD STORY: This is the same as One-Word Story, except it can be two to seven words. You can keep track of the number of words by inconspicuously using your fingers behind your back to keep count.

You will find that, at this point in the exercises, you are more than willing to contribute as much as you can because the restriction of the one word story actually makes you want to talk more. You will also see how easy it is to come up with story lines.

7. STORY, STORY, FRY: The team is placed in a circle (or, if it's a small team of four or five, a straight line). One of the members gets in front of the team or in the middle of the circle and points to the different team members one at a time. As long as the finger is pointed at a specific team member, that team member has to keep a story line going.

The moment the person pointing the finger moves to point to another team member, the team member that was just speaking has to abruptly stop (mid-sentence, mid-word, mid-syllable) and the next team member has to pick up at exactly the same point the first team member left off (without repeating what the previous person said). This continues with the leader randomly pointing to different team members for varying lengths of time, from one second to about twenty seconds.

You have to keep the story continuous without abruptly changing the story line. You cannot hesitate for even a moment. You cannot start rattling off lists of items. You cannot stop until the finger is pointed away from you. If anyone hesitates and loses concentration, they have to sit down because your brain just fried. Whoever is left standing finishes off the story and that's it!

This exercise is designed to stimulate Brain Fry. Some of the best improvisers fry early in the game. The purpose is to short-circuit the brain. This is how we can know we are opening up new neural pathways. If your brain isn't stimulated by now, then someone had better check your pulse. It's fun to try this game at least three times and then take a ten minute break. This will allow your neural pathways to calm down and heal the electrical onslaught.

8. WHAT ARE YOU DOING? This requires two rows of team members facing each other. This time one person from one row starts moving over to the middle of the two rows. This person has to make some kind of unusual type of movement. At this point one person of the second row comes up to the first person in the middle and asks, "What are you doing?" The first person answers by describing something that has absolutely no relationship to their physical actions, and then the two people cross over to the opposing rows to exchange roles when it is their turn later in the sequence.

For example:

A person starts slithering and undulating over to the middle. A second person asks, "What are you doing?" and the first person answers, "I'm making a pizza!"

This exercise is designed to directly access and reinforce Holographic Thinking. It requires you to do two different things at the same time, a great multitasking exercise good for mind expanding.

9. DIFFICULT OFFERS: This is another two-row exercise where the same kind of crossing over of row members occurs as in the "What Are You Doing?" game. This time, however, the first person from row number one gives the person from row number two an imaginary object. This object should be the most awful thing that person can think of. The second person says, "Thank you," and finds some creative way to positively use the object just offered to them.

For example:

The first person pretends to hand the second person a bucket of old, dirty underwear. The second person says to the first, "Thank you, I had a small load of laundry, and I can now fill the washing machine so I wouldn't feel bad for wasting water."

This exercise is designed to show how it is possible to accept and develop any idea positively, which is vital for good teamwork. It is also important, because "The road to great ideas is paved by idiotic ones."

10. FREEZE TAG: Two people start performing a scene with a suggestion of a specific location, or relationship, from the other people who are observing the ones starting the scene. The scene starts out, and then in about ten to twenty seconds, someone says, "Freeze!" The two people performing immediately stop and remain frozen in whatever position they are in.

The person who said "Freeze" has to immediately come over to the original performers, tap one of them on the shoulder so they can sit down, assume the exact position and expression they were in and take the scene in an entirely different direction, while justifying the position they just took.

In a few seconds, a third person says "Freeze" and taps one of the performers on the shoulder and so on repeating this process until everyone is totally exhausted. People can go up over and over again.

For example:

Someone says, "Hi, I'm your sister," and the other performer will accept that, even though they wanted you to be their brother or a tree. Don't say, "No, you're my brother." This exercise is the ultimate in teaching flexibility in visualization. Some of the ground rules are to never negate what anyone offers in a scene and to remember to not say no in the course of a scene.

This is a final set of exercises that will accomplish almost everything necessary for you becoming a more objective thinker. As you do these exercises and become more proficient with them, you will find yourself more and more creatively inspired.

Remember the ten rules of creativity when you are doing any and all of these exercises.

REINVENTING OURSELVES

The main task in staying vital and thinking in new ways is to keep reshaping the imaginary picture of ourselves. In the example of "traveling through space as fast as you possibly can," that imaginary picture has to be revisited frequently. This revisiting is reinventing yourself. As long as we are willing to reinvent ourselves, we can always think in new ways.

When we are no longer willing to allow ourselves to feel uncomfortable by changing the patterns of what we do, true thinking ceases. This is called crystallization, and, as we get older, we are particularly susceptible to this. It really is the end of our originality. That is why you will find so many people, in all different kinds of creative professions, who were once spectacular in what they did but then fade, "lose it," burn out" or retire.

If you want to stay mentally acute, you can't just keep doing the same thing forever, just because it worked for you in the past. The chief reason for creative blocks to thinking more objectively is relying on a limited method of being creative or thinking.

As I have shown, there are many methods to be creative and to think in new ways. However, most people only learn one or two ways. The chief way to reinvent ourselves is by utilizing the new ways of being creative and thinking that have been discussed and, most importantly, to invent your own new ways at looking at things.

SUMMING IT UP

I hope you can begin to understand what it takes to think like Albert Einstein, Leonardo da Vinci and all the other visionary thinkers. I hope you learned what you have to do to think like them and why it is so valuable to think like them.

The time for great thinkers in this world couldn't be more imperative. We all need to help each other out. People, even smart people, are getting duped by new scams every day. We are heading into a world where we soon will not be able to distinguish whether we are running technology or technology is running us. There is almost no education to teach others how to think critically.

The more interconnected the world becomes, the more the usual suspects will feel the need to have more power and control over others. In the past, there was always some kind of frontier to run off to and restart your own culture of some sort. Some place to escape from tyrants. Now that is almost nonexistent. More than ever, it is vital to increase intelligence everywhere as much as possible, so that we do not become manipulated into becoming a giant mechanistic society, not that it isn't that way now, if not worse. See Fritz Lang's 1927 feature length science fiction film *"Metropolis."* It is exactly where we are headed.

If not for yourself, at least for your children and generations to come, it is imperative that some people, even in small numbers, learn how to teach conscious critical thinking.

My purpose in life is to make some meaningful contribution to the evolution of true intelligence and not mistake intelligence for the technology of convenience.

I am still learning. In fact, every time I think I know everything about something, I learn something new. If we don't continue to use and develop our minds, then what is the purpose of humanity in the first place? If we don't evolve mentally, then we are all doomed to be slaves and replaceable machine parts.

The time to take action is now. With society driving us to work so hard to just survive, we have no time to devote to improving our own minds.

ARE YOU YOUR EYES OR THAT WHICH LOOKS OUT OF YOUR EYES?

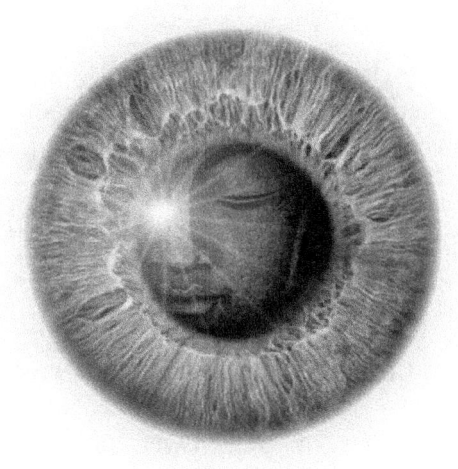

CHECK LIST FOR ACCESSING THE HIGHER MIND

Question everything; don't just believe anything.

Try to be more objective by recognizing Formatory Thinking in yourself.

Dump your mind trash with good humor and eliminate self-judgment. Have a positive self-forgiving attitude.

Become the observer and do not get immersed in success or failure. Be that which looks out of your eyeballs.

Use your peripheral vision, be out of patterns and divide your attention.

Face fears, eliminate negative emotions, and cleanse your magnetic field.

Be aware of your contradictory behavior, accept criticism and learn something from everything.

Dare to Fail, Dare to Start Over, don't wallow in self-pity and make the first thousand mistakes right away.

Use your creative imagination. Increase left/right brain thinking with the brain exercises and warm-up.

Think three dimensionally, channel through the "no thoughts" exercise and don't take credit for what you are channeling.

React naturally and develop your True Personality. Be and express yourself.

Get inspired through creating teamwork buddies and power share with them.

If you can't think of something in the moment, do some improvisational dance movement.

Take in some beauty, be it art or nature.

Don't give up, but you can surrender to the Universe's help, in its typical convoluted way.

COMMENTARY ON MEDIOCRITY

In the process of writing this book, I was discussing and showing parts of it to a person I know in a coffee house I frequent. Another person who also frequents the coffee house, overheard my conversation, was filled with fear and said, "if we open ourselves up too much, evil spirits would occupy our bodies!" I was truly shocked. This, in my opinion, is probably the unhealthiest attitude and the furthest thing from the truth that a person could have.

Evils are born out of repressing our feelings and thoughts, not from facing them. It is fear in itself that justifies the wrongs that people do to each other. Tyrants commit atrocities because of their fears.

"It's not whether a person feels fear or not that defines them. It's what a person does when they feel fear."

This person in the coffee house went on to say, "Some crazy person might read your book and think that they could do anything they want to and kill people."

I asked, "You mean someone else or you?

He apparently had been so repressed in his life that he feared what he would do. The poor guy never had the opportunity to express himself freely, if at all. The irony is that he was more in fear of his imaginary actions, what he would do, than if he had ever had the opportunity to let off some steam and actually express himself.

It is a sad day when we shouldn't publish something or do something that can bring happiness and personal fulfillment, for fear of someone taking it the wrong way. Unfortunately this is more of a common occurrence than one would wish it to be.

This is a tremendously powerful example of why people don't think like Einstein or any other great-minded person.

"DOES FEAR CREATE MEDIOCRITY OR DOES MEDIOCRITY CREATE THE NEED FOR FEAR?"

DEGREES AND LICENSING

It is amazing to me how society has become so fearful of imperfection; that to express yourself for a living has to be associated with a degree of some kind. Think about how Einstein, da Vinci, Shakespeare and Bach, to mention just a few, would have fared in this kind of climate.

Why is it that so many great works of art or great inventions come from people who didn't make it through so-called higher institutions of learning? Even Steve Jobs who changed the world dropped out. Yet so many people pride themselves on a piece of paper that reflects that they sat through and listened to other people's ideas and their own arbitrary tests on their ideas. I reflect back to the incident where my son got a C for expressing himself freely.

This is where this line of thought has gone awry and become formatory. Even though I have both a Master's and Ph.D. degree myself, this only reflects that I learned how to work the system and does not reflect my actual capabilities which are from intuitive life experiences. People mistake degrees for intelligent thinking, but in most cases, they are only a reward for just playing the system and not thinking much at all.

Because a person can speak eloquently, doesn't make them more intelligent. The media is filled with these kinds of people. Look at the news or who has their own TV show. Why do you think we have the kind of governments that we have.

Our present society values fluff and duff over substance.

As I was cooking dinner one evening for some friends, one of them said, "You do so many different things and you can cook too!" This comment struck me as quite odd, because people have always been doing a multiplicity of creative things in their ordinary daily lives and not making a big deal out of it. I discussed this for some time with my friend. he asked something that I think about quite frequently:

"When and how did inventing, creating and thinking about new ideas get separated from our daily lives?"

FINAL THOUGHTS

Most people agree about the incredible intelligence of Einstein.

Since Einstein's brain was dissected and revealed that, he actually had the alert brain of a young man at the time of his death, and that he had a thickening of the corpus callosum, and how this was the physical evidence of such great intelligence, and how his great intelligence towers over most other humans in this world; With this, he had tremendous compassion and he used it for a socially progressive morality.

He was not that concerned with material things and used what he did have to continue to further human knowledge of our purpose on this planet and its place in space and time. He is not the only person that ever lived that had such great intelligence, and who valued knowledge and humanity over greed and obscene opulence, but he is the only one who allowed us to look into his physical brain and see how this intelligence was so, what it had yielded and how it worked.

With all that empirical evidence, wouldn't you think that the world would make a beaten path to understand why and how this kind of intelligence would result in such compassion and social conscience?

And yet, we have the biggest collection of selfish, narrow-minded fools running the affairs of this world. Many of which, in this country, are even hell- bent on restricting the ability of their own people to become educated to be critical thinkers.

As the great philosophical comedian George Carlin said:

"These rulers over us want us just smart enough to run the machines efficiently, but not smart enough to even know how we are enslaved and are continually being enslaved to be ruled by them."

It is not possible to break away from this mental, emotional, physical enslavement unless enough of us learn how to break away from Formatory Thinking and get others to do the same. It is our only true tool to combat these myopic-thinking self-aggrandizing fools.

Why?

It is because, if you have a society that doesn't critically think, the masses can always be manipulated by its rulers by taking their good intentions and turning them into their own opposite. They manipulate the masses by manufacturing false fears through their struggle to survive. This bolsters greed and enslaves the masses.

I feel it has become near impossible to discuss politics with people in general. Why? Because they are so immersed in Formatory Thinking that I can't even begin to get them to understand just the basics of human dignity and evoke the mysterious experience that is so often referred to as common sense. How is it possible to have a discussion when people choose to just believe in things without questioning and believe in those things more than choose to see and understand proven science?

Do you see your beliefs objectively? Or, do your beliefs shape what you see?

Yes, science has its share of flaws, but compared to the plethora of contradictions in most belief systems, science looks almost perfect. The big difference is that science always leaves the door open to new discoveries where belief systems are a closed loop.

Please take to heart this information I present to you and see how it can be applied to yourself, as I do every day myself. Don't just throw it onto the heap of the rest of the pile of drivel which we have become used to having served up to us for breakfast lunch and dinner. Although the brain exercises are fun, humorous and simple, their effects are profound and far reaching.

ABOUT ELLIOT LAURENCE

In addition to a conventional education as an architect and a planner, Elliot has studied Eastern and Western philosophies, psychology and has a PhD in Philosophy. In his twenties, after he and a group of 12 others searched the world for schools of higher knowledge, Elliot Laurence finally discovered some hidden esoteric ideas. He spent many years practicing what he has learned, the first three years of which living in a secluded retreat, just studying and applying its principles.

He has studied, martial arts, Buddhism, Gurdjieff, Ouspensky, Sufism, Gnosticism, Kabala, Esoteric Christianity, *The Egyptian Book of The Dead, the Tibetan Book Of the Dead,* Lao Tzu, *The I Ching* and many others practices and rituals.

Elliot Laurence also has a multifaceted background. He is an architect, designer, inventor, musician, writer, artist, actor, director and teacher. He has won architectural design awards and has worked in the corporate world as CEO of five corporations. He has planned large, projects, including redesigning the Items Processing System for the Bank of America and planning a 1,500-acre destination resort in Northern California. He also provided the concepts for the interiors of two major casinos in Las Vegas.

Elliot has produced commercials and directed an improvisational theater in Las Vegas called "The Grand Order Of Fools (G.O.O.F. Theater). His music has appeared on a nationally syndicated radio show and he has taught improvisational comedy to members of the Las Vegas Screen Actors Guild.
.

In 1991 he received the Educator of the Year award for his teaching methods at the Academy of Art University in San Francisco.   .

He has published four previous books. *The Creative Quotient* (how to reach your full creative potential, *Why Anything Anyway* (The Unified Theory of Conscious Enlightenment), *The Hitchhikers Guide to Enlightenment* (how to not get diverted from your conscious aim, by shiny stuff) and *A 30 Day Economy Fix* (revealing who is stopping the economy from recovering, by showing how it can quickly be fixed)

Through his experiences, Elliot learned how to adapt improvisation theater techniques to develop mind game exercises that can get people to expand their brain's capabilities. As the founder and director of Mindmavericks.org, he is now available to speak for groups and organizations. He may even lead a workshop or two from time to time.

MY PERSONAL JOURNEY

All our knowledge has its origins in our perceptions. "Leonardo da Vinci"

For as long as I can remember, I have been a person who aggressively pursued my creative explorations. I was a musician from age seven, started drawing and building models of different inventions in my preteens and was working in an architecture firm at age seventeen, even before I went to architecture school. I have always had a fascination for science, astrophysics and space. Although I do not have a degree in any of those sciences, I have studied them independently and still do to this day.

I was a professional architectural illustrator. I was also elected educator of the year at the Academy of Art University in San Francisco, for teaching all forms of art and design from drawing, water color, oil, acrylics, mixed media, digital imaging and conceptual design. Yet I still really do not think of myself as an artist because I feel more like an explorer in this life.

Art and design are just tools for me so any subject can be of interest to me, including business. In fact, I have been the CEO of five corporations and did business acquisitions which required me to evaluate all kinds of concerns, from companies in paper and plastic manufacturing to thirty million dollar steel fabricators.

I always try to connect observations. When I was around ten years old and not yet exposed to the study of plate tectonics, I remember looking at a map of the world and thinking to myself, it looks as if Africa fits into the Gulf of Mexico. Maybe they were connected once, but how?

That same year I even wrote a letter to NASA suggesting that instead of using staged booster engines, they use a reusable vehicle. I have made many other observations like that throughout my life. In my youth, I was a bit shy and kept these observations to myself, until I became an adult and developed the self confidence to speak my mind.

There are things that children have clear perceptions of, because no one has censored them yet.

THE GAME CHANGER

A person starts to live when he can live outside himself. "Albert Einstein"

In my early twenties, I took martial arts for about a year. I was sparring in the park with a friend of mine who had introduced me to it and was much better than I was. All of a sudden I had an out-of-body experience, but it is better described as an "*inner*" body experience.

The experience unfolded when I felt as if I was dancing not fighting. My opponent seemed to be moving in slow motion and I was swatting and blocking his kicks and punches, as if redirecting soap bubbles in the air. I was not even looking directly at him. Instead, I was looking up at the trees and surroundings as this was going on.

This lasted for about five minutes and the only reason we stopped was because he got exhausted, where I was still full of energy. He told me later, that at one point, he got really angry and was trying to land real blows.

What I remembered doing prior to this experience was speeding up the perception in my mind as to what I considered fast; how I could react, having fun moving through the feeling of dancing and changing my relationship of what I thought my reaction should be to speed.

The important part of that experience was that I was actually being attacked and was not imagining it.

After that inner body experience, I began a journey of over forty years, to find out what that was all about.

In connecting things as I usually do, I look back and see how this inner body experience was the key and the beginning to my understanding the capabilities of the mind and innovation. I have studied Eastern and Western philosophies and both Einstein and Leonardo da Vinci's lives extensively. To my delight, I realized their brains worked in the way as my research has independently uncovered for.

WHAT HAPPENED AFTER THE INNER BODY EXPERIENCE?

At first I asked everyone I could about the inner body experience, even my seventh generation Japanese karate instructor; he had no answers. Intuitively I stopped my karate classes and learned how to do improvisational comedy. I did not know exactly why then, but I do now. All I knew then was that my inner body experience was generated by my mind's perception and that improv is the martial arts of the mind. Every accomplished martial artist knows that it is a matter of the mind first and then the body follows.

Shortly after completing the improv course, I found myself in a loosely knit group of new friends, from different areas of my life. We all miraculously seemed to come together and meet at that time and place. There were twelve of us and we would meet regularly. There was another architect like myself, three psychiatrists and their wives, a filmmaker and his wife, an engineer and a social worker.

Together we came up with the idea, that there was some hidden knowledge in the world that might be able to not only explain my experiences, but their own unusual experiences. In one of these meetings we decided that we would all go to different places in the world to find this hidden knowledge and meet back in a year. I stayed and explored things in the US and was "contact central," since there was no internet at that time.

We finally all met up eighteen months later. Each of us had amazing experiences and met some very interesting characters and gurus. We shared what we had learned and tried the many things we had discovered from our travels, but nothing really hit the spot and could give us the answers we were looking for. For the most part, it was a lot of hit and miss.

Finally, through someone's common friend, we found a group that was studying about a man that lived in the turn of the century well up into 1949. His name was Gurdjieff. He also had a brilliant collaborator named Ouspensky. Their system of knowledge called "The Fourth Way" really spoke to me.

WHY THE FOURTH WAY?

Before I tell you about The Fourth Way and the other ways, it is important to explain that my interest in The Fourth Way or any of the other ways has been from a scientific self-exploration perspective. Although many people have looked at these things from a spiritual point of view and there is nothing wrong with that, I have always looked at them more scientifically and tried to find practical verifiable applications.

In the past, there were three basic ways of trying to achieve higher consciousness, which is also associated with a spiritual experience. I found it was important to separate higher consciousness and the spiritual experience, because they are, in fact, two separate experiences.

Consciousness is about becoming more self-aware and the cosmos around us. It is more about psychology and self realization. Spirituality is about understanding your own astral body and those of other entities that may or may not exist.

People mix these two ideas up all the time and which is why there is so much confusion and misdirection in the New Age community. However, in history and in the consciousness tradition, there have been three basic paths to conscious enlightenment.

The first way is the way of the Fakir. This way is achieving other dimensional states of consciousness, by overcoming physical pain. Practices like fasting, standing on one leg for hours or days at a time, lying on a bed of nails or other self inflictions have been practiced by both Eastern and Western ideologies.

The second way is the way of the Monk. This is achieving other-dimensional states of consciousness by overcoming emotional pain, through isolation and focus on hard work and toil. Again this is both an Eastern and Western concept. In the East, it is through Buddhist monasteries and martial arts. In the West, it is through priories, monasteries or convents and doing difficult tasks such as writing painstaking books by hand with elaborate illuminations; all done by denying oneself from having personal pleasures, relationships and a family.

The third way is the way of the Yogi. Yogis try to achieve enlightenment through mental denial, meditation and stopping of thoughts. This method is the most popular today in the West. Is can also be used in conjunction with the physical practice of yoga movements, but is primarily a mental practice.

In the Gurdjieff method, it was about taking the all three practices to a whole new level, thus creating The Fourth Way.

The Fourth Way is sometimes nicknamed the "sly mans way." It uses the other ways but in the ordinary conditions of life. For example: I can fast and do a "body cleanse," stop thoughts and achieve a certain kind of altered experience from mental denial and still go to work. I can intentionally avoid a particular relationship and experience emotional denial or keep silent about something for a specific purpose and so forth. This is actually more difficult than the other three ways, because, while it is easy to give up everything once, sequestered in a monastery or a priory, to be in the midst of temptation all the time and have to give up things every day can be excruciating at times.

The most important aspect of The Fourth Way was to show how we are all mechanical stimulus-response machines. That in order to change from being such a machine requires very intentional and persistent efforts, because, as machines, we are so habitual in our behavior that it is near impossible to make these changes in ourselves.

This way was fine and although it clearly showed me how I was a machine, it didn't give me a method to overcome this dilemma without long laborious efforts. I did a lot of psychological experimentation in that group. However, I still could not quite effectively get past the habitual behavior effectively and certainly was not experiencing that inner body experience again.

This changed, when I started doing improv again in the mid 1980's. This time I learned a method of improv, developed by an incredible innovator in this area, Keith Johnstone. He taught a scientific approach to it, which was right up my alley. I took that a step further and through my psychological studies connected his method with the self realization work. This began to effectively get me past mechanical thinking and give me the inner body results I was looking for.

Eventually it resulted in the discovery of what this book is about a "Fifth Way." This is an accelerated way that uses the principles of The Fourth Way, speeds up the process, demystifies things, gives practical tools in our daily lives and scientifically shows you techniques to increase the capabilities of the mind. You do not have to make the process heavy, laborious and serious. You no longer have to set up difficult situations and challenges that create suffering and self denial. Instead, it gets you right to the point, with fun and humor. The only challenge is to your brain. Any difficulties and challenges to overcome in life will occur in normal life circumstances all on their own. The Fifth Way uses the excitement of our own endorphins to overcome our mechanical thinking.

This was a very exhilarating discovery, and, as mentioned previously, although there are a few methods around that try to get you to a state of what is called "Holographic Thinking" through sounds and light, what I am showing you is how to achieve this core experience, under any conditions especially chaotic ones, without contraptions and under your own abilities. Through it, you will always find a way to adapt and create your own specific method when you need it.

ABOUT MENTORS

I could not have had certain breakthroughs if I had not had mentors that helped me see things about myself. Mentors come in all shapes, sizes and temperaments. They even often occur unexpectedly. I have personally had some mentors that were actually quite brutal, unwilling and even deceptive in their approach to teaching but, I was fortunate in three ways:

First, I desired to get what they had to offer even when it was difficult and painful.

Second, I had the ability or some luck that enabled me to separate the useful parts from the non useful parts.

Third, I was able to separate the ideas from the person.

Mythologies are fraught with stories of those seeking a prize object of some sort, symbolizing truth and knowledge. Seekers all had to go through trials and tribulations to get what they sought. This is because, for whatever reason, learning the truth has a cost or sacrifices associated with it. From what I have observed, the reason for this is: without a cost, people simply do not see and appreciate its value.

In the end, they find that what they were seeking is in them already, and the mentor is merely there to just bring that out of them. There is no better example of that than in the story of *The Wizard of Oz.*

Special thanks to:

Danielle Hunter   and   Sue Hines

and their editing skills.

Primarily I am a thinker, writing is the collateral damage.

They both saved the day.

REFRENCES:

The Psychology of Man's Possible Evolution - P.D.Ouspensky

Obedience to Authority- Stanly Millgram

Ted Weekends - Kelly McGonigal TALK

Impro - Keith Johnstone

Tao Tse Ching, - Lao Tsu- Jane English translation

The Quotable Einstein - Alice Calaprice

Dialogues of Plato - http://www.sacred-texts.com/cla/plato/

http://www.carl-jung.net/collective_unconscious.html

The History Channel - Mankind, the story of all of us

History2 Channel - The Universe

History2 Channel - Your bleeped up brain

The Through Wormhole - The Discovery channel

http://en.wikipedia.org/wiki/Holonomic_brain_theory

http://www.stepheerobbins.com/

http://www.messagetoeagle.com/brainholograph.php

http://goertzel.org/dynapsyc/2007/holomind.htm

http://www.statpac.org/walonick/reality.htm